STAND
FIRM

DAVE BRANON

STAND FIRM

48 Life-Guides from Philippians

Discovery House.
from Our Daily Bread Ministries

Stand Firm

© 2014 by Dave Branon

All rights reserved.

Discovery House is affiliated with Our Daily Bread Ministries, Grand Rapids, Michigan.

Requests for permission to quote from this book should be directed to: Permissions Department, Discovery House, P.O. Box 3566, Grand Rapids, MI 49501, or contact us by e-mail at permissionsdept@dhp.org

Interior design by Michelle Espinoza

Library of Congress Cataloging-in-Publication Data
Branon, Dave.
Stand firm : 48 life-guides from Philippians / Dave Branon.
    p. cm.
  ISBN 978-1-57293-815-1
1. Bible. Philippians—Textbooks. I. Title.
  BS2705.55.B73 2014
  227'.606—dc23   2014013047

Printed in the United States of America

Second printing in 2015

CONTENTS

Introduction   7

Philippians 1
Saints, Prayers, Chains, and Worthy Conduct   9

Philippians 2
Humility, Blamelessness, and Personal Business   71

Philippians 3
For Christ, We Press On   113

Philippians 4
Some Teaching, Some Thanking,   155
and a Kind Good-bye

About the Author   215
Note to Reader   216

INTRODUCTION

Can Paul change our lives? Do we want him to?

It's true that the apostle Paul changed the lives of many people in an entire region during his lifetime as he spread the gospel and started churches from Palestine to Rome. But is it possible for his ancient words and two-thousand-year-old ideas to lead us to positive improvements in our lives today? Can this man's thoughts and ideas—inspired though they are—compel us and help us to interact successfully with a world that seems to be increasingly hostile to our faith? And possibly even find ways to change that world?

For us, the mechanism for those possible changes comes from some letters Paul wrote in a far different era to people facing far different problems. Yet in those God-breathed and timeless words are found the seeds for spiritual growth that can bring renewal and encouragement to our twenty-first century lives.

When we read Paul's letter to his brothers and sisters in the faith at Philippi, we are eavesdropping on a personal note to some people who were extremely important in the apostle's life. One evidence of their importance is the fact that Paul used first person pronouns about a hundred times in this short letter. This wasn't because Paul was bragging or self-centered but because he was penning a letter to people he knew cared for him and who would understand the problems he was experiencing. Just as we love getting personal notes from those we love, they wanted to hear about him and about how his situation could inform, guide, and shape their lives as followers of Christ. He also knew they would listen carefully to the hopes he had for them.

As we listen in, we can hear what true Christian love sounds like and what fellowship in the gospel can mean to a group of people focused on a single cause and energized by a single Savior.

The gospel of Jesus Christ had changed the lives of the people in this church Paul had helped start one Sabbath day beside the river Gangites outside the walls of Philippi, and because of their changed lives they had supported Paul and encouraged him in his ministry. Now, as he wrote this letter to them, they could learn secondhand some of the valuable lessons Paul had learned firsthand through the tough times he had endured as a missionary. And because God preserved this letter for us, we too can see how Paul's life was used for God's glory, how he expected that to be duplicated in the church at Philippi, and how that can spill over to us today.

Indeed, Paul's words can change our lives as he reminds us what it means to live for God, trust in God, and find an inexplicable peace in Jesus Christ despite the irritating and challenging realities of our highly secular world.

PHILIPPIANS 1

SAINTS, PRAYERS, CHAINS, AND WORTHY CONDUCT

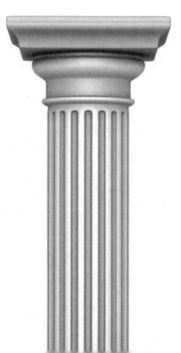

PHILIPPIANS 1:1–2

Paul and Timothy, bondservants of Jesus Christ,
to all the saints in Christ Jesus who are in Philippi,
with the bishops and deacons: Grace to you and peace
from God our Father and the Lord Jesus Christ (NKJV).

What You Need To Know

The book of Philippians is a letter penned by a man charged with something that was bad enough to get him incarcerated. Imagine what some church people today might say if the congregation received a similar letter from someone in prison who was audacious enough to make suggestions about how the church folk should be living. More than a few of them would probably be upset, or at least taken aback, by this man's authoritative tone.

But there's something quite different going on here. The writer of this letter, Paul, was imprisoned (or, more likely, under house arrest) not for theft or extortion or murder, but for doing what all of us should be doing: He was trying to get the gospel of Jesus Christ out to those who needed to hear it.

Paul told the people at Philippi about that when he said, "It has become clear throughout the whole palace guard and to everyone else that I am in chains for Christ" (vv. 13–14). This was not some excuse from a guilty man to make himself look good. Paul was indeed being persecuted for his faith and his faithfulness—and that's definitely not a crime that would disqualify him from giving advice and help to his contemporaries or to us.

Perhaps we can look at it this way: Paul's prisoner status made him the perfect teaching example for us all. It's as if he could say, "Look, if I can go through this for Jesus, you can be more courageous than ever before in telling others about Him."

Encouragement and instruction from a brave prisoner for Jesus. That's what this book is about.

Servant or Saint?

Sometimes there is nothing better for the people in the church than to see their pastor with a hammer in hand helping add a new wall to the church nursery. Or walking behind a lawn mower cutting the church lawn. Or wielding a shovel to help keep the church sidewalk clear of snow.

A pastor willing to exert a little elbow grease like this understands something important that Paul made clear as he opened his letter to the Philippians: Leadership requires servanthood. He and Timothy—men everyone in the young church of their day recognized to be leaders, mentors, and missionaries—were to be viewed as servants. And the readers of this epistle—the people to whom Paul addressed this inspired note of thanks and exhortation—were the saints.

Consider what this means: Leaders as servants and the church crowd as saints. Think about what might change at your church if things were viewed this way by all.

Notice as well that although Paul would mention many areas of concern later in his letter, in his greeting he was not asking anything of these people. As a true servant leader, he was offering them something of inestimable value: grace and peace.

We call him Paul the Apostle, but here he is Paul the Servant. Wouldn't it be an honor to have that title!

What a statement we would make to our circle of friends, both Christians and non-Christians, if they were to recognize us as true, humble servants—if they knew that if a job needed to be done, we would be there to do it without fanfare or hope of recognition.

This should also encourage us to pray even more diligently that those who have leadership roles both in the local church and in other organizations throughout the Christian community would embrace this challenge to lead by serving. We have all watched in embarrassment and disillusionment as Christian leaders have overstepped their bounds by seeking power—power of money, power of prestige, or power of influence—instead of service. We know how much it hurts the mission of the church when they misuse their authority in this way.

The opening words of the imprisoned apostle should remind us to recognize the godly strength behind servanthood, no matter which saint we are: leader or layperson. After all, a greater example than even Paul—our Lord himself—was said to have strived "not to be served, but to serve" (Mark 10:45).

Like Jesus. Like Paul. Like the snow-shoveling pastor. Let's strive to be saints who are servants living in the glow of God's grace and peace—not in the spotlight of human attention.

How Do These Verses Help Me Stand Firm?

It can help me to think of which person I am in this verse. If I am a leader, then I can lead by serving. If I am not in leadership, then I need to serve with humility in whatever position God has called me to fill.

What Has to Change?

Is my life marked by grace? Is my life marked by peace? Am I a "lord it over people" leader, or can I learn to be a servant leader?

PHILIPPIANS 1:3-5

I thank my God every time I remember you. In all my prayers for all of you, I always pray with joy because of your partnership in the gospel from the first day until now.

What You Need To Know

It's called "the book of Philippians," but for a lot of people, Philippians is kind of a mystery word. What is a Philippian? Is it a person? Where does a Philippian live? Why does it begin with "Ph"?

A Philippian is a person who lived in the city of Philippi. Think about the present country of Greece, move north on the Aegean Sea between all the islands, go northwest past the peninsula that contains Mt. Athos, and travel until you hit land. Inland just a few miles is where Philippi was located.

Philippi was a Roman colony, and it was here that Paul and Silas were tossed into prison for casting a demon out of a little girl.

Luke describes the beginnings of the church in Philippi in Acts 16. Lydia, a woman who sold purple cloth for a living, seems to have been the first convert, and it was in her home that the church later met.

While Paul was on a missionary journey after the Philippian church was established, a man named Epaphroditus delivered a gift to him from the church in support of his ministry. Subsequently, Paul took the opportunity to send back with Epaphroditus a letter thanking the people and guiding them with spiritual advice. We call that letter "Philippians."

Endless Prayer? Seriously?

Did you ever read the advice of experts and think, "Yeah, right! That's impossible."

Like when you read a handyman magazine article that gives twenty-five ways to cut your electricity bill, but all it does is remind you that you hardly know how to turn the lights off and on—let alone install the dimmer switches the article is suggesting so you can cut your bill by 3 percent.

Or when you read a financial wizard's plan to get out of debt and live the rest of your life on easy street. And you think, "Uh, have you ever seen my checkbook?"

Impossible, you think.

And then you read Philippians 1:3, and you feel as if you have been beamed right back into the land of make-believe. Sure, Paul. Easy for you to say.

Think about how difficult it would be to actually do as Paul suggested: "I thank my God every time I remember you." Imagine that every time you think about your husband, your wife, your son, your daughter, your best friend you offer up a prayer of thanks on their behalf.

Every time. Like just right there when you read "husband, wife, son, daughter, best friend," did you do it?

Not easy.

If we could actually accomplish that goal, it would do one of two things: we would either start being extremely prayerful or we would actively try to stop thinking about that person as much. Too much effort!

But Paul didn't stop with just a promise to pray—although that's what most of us would probably do. For instance, how often do we dutifully and honestly promise to pray for a need someone has? But then we get busy or distracted or tired and that prayer promise goes the way of last week's grocery list—forgotten.

While we don't have a record of how Paul did with his audacious prayer promise, we can guess, from knowing what we learn about him in the rest of the New Testament, that he followed through. But he offered more than just the promise. He actually gave an outline of what those prayers would be.

In verses 9–11 Paul detailed four things he would pray about as he sent out his God-directed pleas for his friends:

- abounding love,
- depth of insight that would lead to discernment,
- pure and blameless living,
- the fruit of righteousness.

With Paul's dedication to specific, promised prayer, he reminds us what a powerful and important tool it is. Prayer is a spiritual discipline that leads to joy—and to amazing connection between us and God.

Stop for a moment and begin to make a list of the people who have a "partnership in the gospel" with you and can make a difference in our world. Think of the difference it would make if you were to be in continual and frequent prayer for them and for some of the following:

- Your pastor as he provides spiritual, servant leadership for your church.
- Christian teachers you know who are making a difference in the lives of young people—men and women who understand that the younger generation is fighting a tough battle against an ungodly world system.
- Young people you know. Pray for them and let them know that you are talking to God about them and that you would love to hear prayer requests from them.
- Leaders in the community and in the nation that you know share a committed faith in Jesus. Pray for wisdom as they seek to make a difference.

Is it possible for us to follow Paul's example by making thankfulness for our fellow Christians and joyful prayer for them as natural as our next breath? Can we send up a prayer—even if it is a short one—every time we think of the people we know who are doing the work of the kingdom? Let's give it a try.

It's much more important than saving on our electric bill or getting out of debt (which most of us aren't very good at anyway). And it's one more way to show our heavenly Father that we trust Him and want all glory and honor and trust to go from our lips to His throne.

How Do These Verses Help Me Stand Firm?

It can keep me in continual contact with God. If thankful prayer—communication with Him—is just a thought away, then using Paul's method will keep that circuit open at all times. It also helps us understand 1 Thessalonians 5:17: "Pray continually."

What Has to Change?

Do I think "thanks" when I think of others, or do I think, "What's his/her problem?" Am I convinced that regular, ongoing prayer for fellow Christians can help change our world for the better?

PHILIPPIANS 1:6

*He who began a good work in you will carry
it on to completion until the day of Christ Jesus.*

What You Need to Know

Paul uses the term "the day of Christ" three times in
the book of Philippians. In addition to using it in chapter
1, verse 6, he also employs it in verse 10 and in chapter
2, verse 16. In fact, it's a term that appears at least ten
times in the New Testament. It is variously referred to
as "the day of our Lord Jesus" (1 Corinthians 1:8), "the
day of the Lord" (1 Thessalonians 5:2; 2 Thessalonians
2:2), and "this day" (1 Thessalonians 5:4). It is generally
accepted that this refers to the day of Jesus' return—when
His glory will be revealed and when He will be united
with His bride, the church. On that day Jesus will be
manifested in glory.

When that day arrives, we will know that the work of
the gospel of Jesus has been completed in this world. This
is the day all of us who have been redeemed by our Savior
are eagerly anticipating. It is the consummation day for
our faith, our work, and our dedication to our Lord.

The Project That Never Ends

When I visited a number of cathedrals in the United Kingdom—from the Worcester Cathedral to Westminster Abbey to St. Mungo in Edinburgh—one thing that stood out to me was that these edifices built to glorify God seemed to be continually under re-construction, renovation, and repair. Construction of some of these buildings began as long as a thousand years ago, but keeping these magnificent cathedrals in repair continues today. Scaffolding seemed to be as prevalent as icons in these ancient buildings.

All around these cathedrals, however, the times have changed. Modern roads and twenty-first century buildings exist in proximity to these churches built generations ago. So in order for them to continue to have an impact on the community that keeps growing and changing, workers are busy updating and maintaining them. Keeping the cathedrals in working order is a project that never ends.

While none of us will be around for another thousand years here on earth, there is something about those cathedrals that is very much like us: We need continual work in our lives to make us presentable and usable for God's glory if we are going to have an impact. We cannot think that once we are "built," or redeemed, we can sit idle amid the ongoing changes of our lives. Like the edifices I saw in England and Scotland, we still need "Pardon our dust" signs, indicating that there is repair work being done.

Paul said it like this: "He [God] who began a good work in you will carry it on to completion [the work will keep going] until the day of Christ Jesus."

While we are made complete in Christ and are considered ready for heaven the moment we put our faith in Him, that does not mean we are immediately complete and perfect in this life.

We have attitudes that lead to ugly stains, which need to be cleaned out of our lives.

We have sins that have to be sandblasted away.

We have prejudices that must be trimmed off and thrown away.

We allow bad habits to creep into our lives, and those habits can cause damage if we don't get rid of them.

We make hurtful statements or speak unfortunate words that must be chipped away with Jesus' forgiveness.

Even our foundation needs to be shored up occasionally by reminders of Christ's faithfulness in our lives. And by God's grace, each of us is still being transformed, being changed by the power of the Holy Spirit in our lives.

The scaffolding of God's grace continues to shore us up. But it's not so we can look good or so others can be impressed with our magnificence. No, when the Spirit of God builds us up, He does so to enable us to carry on His work.

Some have the idea that the work of God in our lives is done so we can be blessed, so we can have favor, so our lives can be made easier. While we do enjoy an abundant spiritual life because of our faith, the more accurate reason for God's work in us is so that we can give glory to God. We are Christ's light in the world, and our purpose is to shine the focus on Him, not on us. That "good work" mentioned in Philippians 1:6 is anything we can do to redirect the attention of the world from self-centeredness and self-indulgence to the One who selflessly came to earth to live and die for us—Jesus.

As we grow closer to that day when time will be no more, we should move toward completeness, maturity, and Christlikeness—

traits that will become manifest in our lives on the day of Jesus Christ. And the more we reflect those traits through God's repair and construction work in our lives now, the bigger impact we will have on the people who populate our world.

Like an old cathedral, we stand firm. We sense that God is still working on us, still finishing us, still pulling us with His power toward that moment when we will begin an eternal celebration of grace through our Savior.

"Pardon my dust," but God is still working on me.

How Does This Verse Help Me Stand Firm?

When I get a little discouraged because I mess up, it's great to know that God's not going to abandon me. And there's a certain confidence in knowing that eventually, on "the day," we win! Isn't it a powerful incentive to keep ourselves under good repair, knowing that God has left us here so we can work toward the consummation that He has planned?

What Has to Change?

I have to stop trying to make needed changes by myself. It's a divine-human cooperative, and God is actively helping me honor Him with my life.

PHILIPPIANS 1:7

All of you share in God's grace with me.

What You Need to Know

Sometimes we get wrapped up in superstar Christianity. No naming names here, but you know who we prop up on the pedestals of our sanctified imagination. Maybe it's famous people who write popular Christian books. Maybe it's top-of-the-line preachers who speak to thousands with smooth and graceful and clever words. Or it could be up-front people at your church. Worship leaders. Musicians. Elders. Others whose names everybody knows.

But that's not how things are intended to be in God's kingdom. There is no hall of fame at the foot of the cross. There, before our suffering Savior, we are all equal. We are all lost sinners who dumped our sins on Jesus and sent Him to die in our stead on a crude hunk of wood.

Even the best-dressed, smoothest, autograph-signing superstar Christian is nothing but a wretched sinner Jesus dragged off the scrap heap of humanity and redeemed through His blood. That person and you and I are as equal as the angles in an equilateral triangle.

You know that part in the great song of the faith "Amazing Grace" where we sing, "Amazing grace—how sweet the sound that saved a wretch like me"? Did you ever stumble over that "wretch like me" a little bit or look around to see if some of the "important people" might have swallowed that word a little instead of singing it out? Well, the hymn writer, that old former slave-trader John Newton, got it right. We are each so wretched that if it were not for God's grace to us, we wouldn't have a prayer.

Without Jesus, all we have to offer are the filthy rags of our sin—no matter who we are.

"It is by grace you have been saved, through faith—and this is not from yourselves, it is the gift of God—not by works, so that no one can boast," says Ephesians 2:8–9. Grace makes us all equal. Boasting just makes us look foolish in the shadow of the cross.

Here, Have Some Grace

Is sharing grace anything like borrowing faith?

I wonder, because a few years ago I discovered a song on Christian radio that floored me with its mystery. The song said something like, "If your faith fails, you can borrow mine." The more I tried to fit those lyrics into what I knew about faith in Jesus Christ, the more I was convinced that faith is not transferable—that it cannot be lent or borrowed.

So then we come upon this verse, which discusses grace-sharing, not faith-borrowing, and somehow it doesn't sound as problematic. Indeed, it sounds like a pretty good idea.

But what does it mean? How did the people of the church in Philippi share in God's grace with Paul? And how do we share it with others? And what difference does this make in a world that is increasingly graceless? How do we share grace?

In the case of the Philippians, they shared grace through their actions. Remember that Paul was in prison—locked away because of his diligent witness for Christ. And while he was there, the church did not forget about him nor did they treat him as an outcast because of his incarceration. Instead, they continued to serve him and identify with him and help him financially. They were conduits of God's grace as it flowed from them to their helpless friend. They were partners in fellowship with their jail-bound comrade in Rome.

For us, this seems to indicate that we should eagerly involve ourselves in the lives of others. And it's rather clear that sharing in God's grace is not something done from the sidelines.

- Grace-sharing means visiting an elderly person in the hospital or nursing home. Nothing says grace more than helping the helpless.
- It means assisting a family financially when joblessness threatens to rob them of their dignity as it sucks their bank account dry. Nothing says grace more than giving sacrificially of our means to buoy up those in need.
- It means putting an arm around a struggling teenager and telling him you love him. Nothing says grace more

than reaching into an unfamiliar world and being Jesus
to the confused.

- It means looking over the horizon of your friends' lives
and seeing who is hurting because of a devastating loss.
Grace encourages you to make that phone call or send
that card. Grace challenges you to reach out to a griev-
ing family to see what needs you can meet—or just to
show them that you care.

God's grace is often defined as His giving us what we don't
deserve. And indeed grace falls on us like rain from above, straight
from God's hand to ours—unregulated by our worthiness. But
as we begin to count the blessings of His grace in our lives, how
appropriate it is to look up from our counting and see who in our
circle of fellow travelers needs to have some of that grace spilled
over into their lives.

There's no mystery about how this happens. It takes interaction from one believer who wants to let his or her overflowing cup
tip some of God's goodness on to another.

We know what grace-sharing is, so the only mystery might be
why we don't do it more often.

How Does This Verse Help Me Stand Firm?

Doesn't this remind me that I am not alone—that I have a
grace-directed fellowship with people who are charged with caring for me, praying for me, and encouraging me? Who are some
special people I share in God's grace with? Think of all the ways
my heart is bound together with others by that grace.

What Has to Change?

Could it be that I've seen God's grace as an individual thing—that God saved me, and that's all I need to know? How can I go from a Lone Ranger Christian to a Go-Team! Christian?

PHILIPPIANS 1:8

God can testify how I long for all of you
with the affection of Christ Jesus.

What You Need to Know

This is one of those verses that those of us who grew up on or still enjoy the King James Version might get a little uneasy about when we read it, because it reads a little too much like a study of the gastrointestinal system. It seems those old-school translators had a struggle trying to properly explain some Bible words that in the Greek appeared to be talking about a person's inner parts. When they got to the word that is translated "affection" here, they chose the word "bowels." So the KJV says, "How greatly I long after you all in the bowels of Jesus Christ."

Paul, it appears, was aiming for a strong word that suggested affection or caring. When we really love something or have intense feelings for someone or some event, something happens in our "inner parts." Nerves. Love. Fright. Anticipation. They all can have that effect. So Paul chose a word that, five hundred years ago, was translated

as "bowels." Today, we call it "affection." But now you
know that it is a deep, stomach-crunching feeling.

You Can Ask God

I recall a time years ago when my seven-year-old son and I
were having a bit of a conflict about something he had done, and
I felt he was not leveling with me. Steve told me one version of
the incident (a positive event in his eyes), but I was pretty sure it
had happened a far different way (a negative event to my way of
thinking). He was convinced his version was right—so much so
that when I pressed him about it, he pulled out the biggest trump
card he could find in his deck of proofs.

"You can ask God about it," he said. "He'll tell you what I did."

I wasn't expecting that! And I didn't know what to say. When
your second-grader calls God to the witness stand to support his
case, it kind of makes you stop and rethink your position.

I'm sure Steve didn't get this defense strategy from his teachers at Sunday school or from the Christian elementary school he
was attending, but it is indeed a biblical notion. And I took it
as a sign that he was extremely serious about his position on the
matter.

Calling on God as a witness in an argument can be found
several times in the pages of God's Word. Of course, Paul does
it in Philippians 1:8 as a way of telling the people how much he
cares for them. He seems to be saying something like this: "I care
for you so very much—and if you need to have someone to verify
this, you can ask God himself. He knows, and He will vouch for
me."

It reminds me a little of what we do in a courtroom. Each witness must swear—or make an oath while touching a Bible—that what he or she says is truth, "so help me God." We operate under the theory that no person of character would dare lie after acknowledging that God is listening in to the proceedings. This is our best human effort to hold a person accountable for his words.

Look at some other times this idea is used in the Bible:

"You know we never used flattery, nor did we put on a mask to cover up greed—God is our witness" (1 Thessalonians 2:5).

"God, whom I serve in my spirit in preaching the gospel of his Son, is my witness how constantly I remember you" (Romans 1:9).

"I call God as my witness—and I stake my life on it—that it was in order to spare you that I did not return to Corinth" (2 Corinthians 1:23).

Paul was so desperate to let his friends in Philippi know how much he cared for them that he summoned the No. 1 witness of all time: his heavenly Father. And he used a term that spoke of deep, inner affection.

You may not call on God to testify as my son wanted to do, but He *is* your witness. Does He see that you have a love for your fellow believers that goes beneath the surface and touches your inner being? Do those you care for know how deep your love is for them?

How Does This Verse Help Me Stand Firm?

From such a short verse I can learn a lot about how important Christian fellowship and concern for those with whom I worship should be. It reminds me how important love for my fellow believers is in God's eyes. This is a challenge to be able to say of my friends, "I care deeply for you."

What Has to Change?

Is my life so wrapped up in my own things that I don't show love for others? Can I take an extra moment to encourage a colleague at work? Write a quick e-mail to someone who needs a boost? Go out to lunch with a hurting friend?

PHILIPPIANS 1:9

*And this is my prayer: that your love may abound more
and more in knowledge and depth of insight.*

What You Need to Know

The apostle Paul mentions prayer more than twenty-five times in his letters preserved in the New Testament. He talks about faithfulness in prayer (Romans 12:12). He mentions some prayers that he had for others (2 Corinthians 13:9, Colossians 4:12; Philippians 1:9). He reminds his readers to be devoted to prayer (1 Corinthians 7:5; Colossians 4:2).

In his letters, Paul always included instruction about, challenges to, or results from prayer. But perhaps nothing shows Paul's faith in talking to God more than his short note at the end of Philemon: "And one more thing: Prepare a guest room for me, because I hope to be restored to you in answer to your prayers" (v. 22). "You are praying, Philemon, so get a room ready." That's confidence. That's Paul knowing that his friend's prayer would be answered. Paul didn't just talk about prayer in his letters. He practiced it, and he knew it was effective in others.

Love Supplements

Did I read that right? Did Paul really pray that his love for the people at Philippi should be characterized by more knowledge and more depth of insight?

I thought love was all mushy and warm and fuzzy. That it had to do with kissing babies, buying flowers for your wife, and whispering sweet somethings into the ear of someone special. Love is indeed a many-splendored thing, but is it really about knowing more stuff and sharpening your insightfulness?

Love, it appears, is not a stagnant pond of emotion. It is a stream of refreshment that grows into a river of knowledge and flows into an ocean of insight. Love expands and widens as it is fed by the knowledge of God's will (Colossians 1:9), the knowledge of God's greatness, and the understanding of Christ's wide, long, high, and deep love for us (Ephesians 3:18).

This knowledge of love, of which Paul speaks, is a never-ending quest. And along the journey of life we experience a wide range of the manifestations of this all-important emotion: our demonstration of love for others by word and deed, God's endless supply of love for us, Christ's boundless love for those for whom He died, and the Spirit's compelling love for those in whom He dwells.

That is how love abounds—how it grows and how it colors our world with a multitude of positive thoughts, actions, and feelings. Stop for a few moments to contemplate the terms of love as spelled out in Scripture.

Love never fails.

God's love will follow us all the days of our lives.

God's love is better than life.

Love covers all wrongs.

Love the Lord with all your heart, soul, and mind.

Love your neighbor as yourself.

Let us love one another.

Whoever lives in love lives in God.

If we have not love, we have nothing.

"By this all men will know that you are my disciples, if you love one another" (John 13:35).

Love, dcTalk once wrote for one of its songs, is a verb. But it is more. Love is a testimony.

Sadly, because of the intense interest many Christians have shown in vital political issues over the past few decades and because of the way they have held forth on controversial issues that affect the way life is lived in our world today, there is an impression out there that Christians are anything but loving. Christians are considered strident and unbending and intolerant.

Unfortunately, those are not characteristics that suggest love.

What we need to do, then, is to find ways to express our convictions while displaying the love that will help others see that we are Jesus' disciples. But isn't that exactly what Paul is talking about? That true, godly love moves us toward a maturity that allows us to be insightful, to be knowledgeable, and to be winsome.

The world outside the church doors needs to see a mature love from those who follow Jesus. It needs to see love as a testimony that Jesus changes hearts into vessels of compassion and that spiritual transformation gives minds greater wisdom and clarity.

Think of the difference we could make in our world if we were to be seen as both intelligent and loving. Isn't that what having our "love abound more and more in knowledge and depth of insight" looks like?

In the letter Paul wrote to the Ephesians, he said, "Follow God's example, therefore, as dearly loved children and walk in the way of love, just as Christ loved us and gave himself up for us as a fragrant offering and sacrifice to God" (5:1–2). To love as Paul describes, we must love as God loves—unselfishly and sacrificially. That is the kind of knowledge that can help set us apart as people of love.

How Does This Verse Help Me Stand Firm?

It is possible to think I have love for God and others without understanding what that really means. However, if I grasp the knowledge and insight that marks true godly love, imagine how that would affect my treatment of others and my affection toward our heavenly Father. Loving as Paul tells me to love could be revolutionary.

What Has to Change?

Do I love for what I can get, or do I love for what I can give? If I love as God loves—who loved me while I was abhorrent and ugly—I will see that my heart-care for others is all about them and their good, not my own. Maybe my attitude has to change if I am to truly love.

PHILIPPIANS 1:12

*What has happened to me has
actually served to advance the gospel.*

What You Need To Know

Imagine for a moment that you were a school friend
of a kid named Saul who lived in Tarsus, in the Roman
province of Cilicia. You both went to a top-notch school
because Tarsus was noted for its fine educational insti-
tutions. You remember how Saul was a sold-out Pharisee, even as a kid. His parents were pretty strict about
their beliefs, so he worked hard to keep the law. You
figured someday he might become one of the leaders
in the synagogue, wearing the fancy garb of religious
power. You watched with a little bit of envy as he began
to study under Gamaliel, one of the most beloved rabbis.
As you got older, you noticed that Saul had become so
entrenched in his faith that when he observed that troublesome new sect of people who believed that Jesus was
the risen Messiah—well, he began to cause trouble for
them. He thought he was doing God's will by his actions,

which culminated in his participation in the stoning of a guy named Stephen.

That was Saul—a hater of Christians and a legalistic Jew to the core. If you were making up a person to be the antagonist in a novel about the young Christian church, you couldn't do better than to create Saul. But your novel would have to take a major turn in the plot, for Saul turned out to be the greatest missionary for the Christian faith the world has ever known. And as it further turns out, he recognized that everything that ever happened to him "served to advance the gospel." But this is no novel. This is the New Testament. You can't make this kind of thing up.

After the Tough Times, Then What?

Life sometimes stinks. It rises up and kicks us in the teeth, leaving us writhing on the ground in pain. When it does, we have two options—two possible reactions.

My wife and I often discuss how things have turned out for us, and we wonder why it had to be that way. When we married, Sue and I, two kids from strong Christian families, had visions of following God's guidelines for raising a family marked by joy and godliness. And that was how things went for a nice long time. I can't say it was ever especially easy. We both worked extremely hard to make sure our four kids were well taken care of spiritually, emotionally, and physically. Money was always tight, and so were our schedules as we worked extra jobs and got extra education to make sure we could provide what we thought were essentials for our children. Yet despite the pressures and challenges, we pressed on with the joy of knowing we were doing things the way we felt God wanted us to do them.

But doing our best as Christian parents to nurture our four children toward godly success didn't turn out exactly how we thought it would. No prayer we prayed, no lesson we taught, no God-centered plans we made could prevent an unspeakable tragedy that visited us in June 2002—and has never left. On a beautiful, warm spring day we lost one-quarter of our hearts when our seventeen-year-old daughter Melissa was killed in a car accident.

As the days of our grief progressed after Melissa died, it became decision time. Those two aforementioned options lay before us. We could either see this as a "kick in the teeth" from God, sending us down a road of godlessness and chaos, or we could see it as an unbearable tragedy (which it is) that could "serve to advance the gospel." We could try to emulate Paul, who started out so successfully as a devoted, legalistic Jew only to switch over to Jesus' side and suffer innumerable difficulties. Yet after he became a follower of Christ, which led to his being thrown in jail and shipwrecked and threatened by mobs, he didn't sit around and pout about things not going his way or wishing he were still dragging away Christians to trial. Instead, no matter what happened to him to send his plans off kilter or to send his worn-out body to prison, he did something counterintuitive. He always pointed back to Jesus. He always remained faithful. He kept on singing and praising.

As best we can, we have chosen Paul's attitude: we are seeking ways to use Melissa's well-lived life and surprising death to point others toward God—from assisting other bereaved people to sharing godly insights whenever possible with teens, who represent our missing daughter.

This has not insured a release from the burden of our pain (as I'm sure it didn't with Paul either), but it has allowed us to know that Melissa—even in her death—can continue to touch lives. And it allows us to have a purpose that could never be fulfilled by wallowing in pity.

Life sometimes stinks.

But we can't let it dictate how we should live. That is the job of the Holy Spirit as our lives are informed by the pages of Scripture. That's why a verse such as 2 Corinthians 2:3 jumps off the pages for us now: "I wrote as I did, so that when I came I would not be distressed by those who should have made me rejoice. I had confidence in all of you, that you would all share my joy." It informs us that God has comforted us so we can give aid to others—and that can only happen by the power of the Spirit. Believe me, it's not our doing, because sometimes we'd much rather curl up and shut out the world that continues to carry on without Melissa.

As each of us finds ways to allow our troubles to be used to lead others to godliness, we can make life a rich aroma of Christ, which seems like a great way to "advance the gospel."

How Does This Verse Help Me Stand Firm?

Nobody wants to waste their time, their energies, their talents, or even their loved ones. When I am smacked in the face with a tragedy, I want that horrible situation to have value. This verse helps me see that in God's way of looking at things the bad things that happen to good people are all part of the good things

God has going in this world. My job is to help those struggles advance the gospel instead of leading me into retreat.

What Has to Change?

Sometimes my pain blocks me from having an attitude that can reflect God's goodness in tough times. So I need to talk to God and ask Him to help me not have the kind of bitterness that blocks His work through tough circumstances.

PHILIPPIANS 1:14

*Because of my chains, most of the brothers and sisters
have become confident in the Lord and dare
all the more to proclaim the gospel without fear.*

What You Need To Know

Chains. It's hard to miss them in this letter. Verse 7:
"I am in chains." Verse 13: "I am in chains." Verse 14:
"my chains." Verse 17: "I am in chains." But although
Paul was "in chains," meaning he was in jail in Rome,
this was not your typical jail. Actually, he lived in a house
rented at his own expense (Acts 28:30), and he was able
to "live by himself," although he had a guard constantly
with him (28:16). Whether Paul meant that he was literally "in chains" or was simply being detained by his
constant guard is unclear. Gordon Fee, in his book *Paul's
Letter to the Philippians*, explains it in these simple terms:
"He is not free to roam about."

The "brothers and sisters" Paul refers to were people
who had come to Christ through his witness after he
arrived in Rome and before he was incarcerated. When

the Jewish people in Rome asked Paul to explain his views, he preached to them, and "some were convinced" and "others would not believe" (see Acts 28). Paul said he would proclaim the gospel to the Gentiles, and for the next two years in Rome he did so. It would seem, then, that the fellow believers he is speaking about in Philippians 1:14 were both Jewish and Gentile converts.

My Bad; Their Good

This is not easy—this idea that Paul is suggesting in Philippians 1:14. Basically, he is saying that when a bad thing happens to us, it's all to the good if that bad thing enables others to witness more boldly or trust God more securely or worship Him more freely.

How hard is that?

It is this hard: It's having to admit that something good—something godly, something eternally powerful—can come from our tough times. Sometimes we'd almost rather chew on nails than say to God that the trouble we are going through is "no problem" if it helps someone else spiritually. There is something in us that wants to say, "It's all about me. And if 'me' is having difficulty, this can't be good."

This runs directly counter to a common way of thinking in the Christian community that says it is God's job to make sure we have smooth sailing—which is a rather revealingly ironic metaphor if you read Acts 27 about Paul's harrowing sailing trip to Rome. Paul seemed never to have smooth sailing as a missionary, literally or figuratively.

If Paul had thought the way so many twenty-first century Christians think, perhaps this is what he would have written in Philippians 1: "Hey, Paul here. As you know, I'm stuck in prison, and it's not pretty. Did you know that I am tethered to a guard all the time? I can't even go to the . . . oh, well, you don't need to know that. And the food. Awful. Most of the time I don't feel like eating. And these guards. They really should consider taking a bath sometime. This is no fun at all. Sure wish I had never come to Rome. A lot of good it's done me to be a missionary!"

What if Paul had written something like that as he awaited his release from jail and his upcoming trial? What if he had spent his precious words calling attention to himself? How would that have helped the folks at Philippi? How would that have encouraged them?

It wouldn't, of course, so the Holy Spirit directed him to take a far different approach. He wanted us to know that God's plans sometimes call for us to endure hardships for His glory. And during good times or bad, our response to our circumstances must be to celebrate our great God. Sometimes it is the will of God for us not to get everything we pray for, not to have the smooth life we desire, not to be free of difficulty and pain.

How many times have we heard someone proclaim that "God is good" because He spared them from some impending difficulty?

"I got the report back from the doctor, and *I'm all clear*. God is good."

"I just *got a big raise*. Isn't God great?"

"I totaled my car, and *should have been injured but wasn't*. Isn't the Lord awesome!"

Indeed God is good, great, and awesome. But that does not change if those outcomes in italics had been "I'm terminal," "got fired," and "was seriously injured." Sometimes God allows "chains" of various kinds to interrupt our lives to encourage others and so that He can receive miraculous honor.

This reminds me of Nick Vujicic. You cannot listen to this man describe with joy and confidence his unflinching faith in God without being deeply challenged. He has for years toured widely proclaiming his faith and encouraging people to overcome. And what trouble has Nick Vujicic experienced that would allow him to lift others up with his compelling story?

Let's start with the fact that he was born without arms or legs. This man could not even wear the chains that Paul spoke about, but his difficulties have had the same effect on others as Paul's prison challenge. How can we not "proclaim the gospel without fear" after hearing Nick say with a conviction that assuredly comes from the Holy Spirit: "I am the richest man on the earth!"

"Standing" on a table so the audience can see him, he goes on: "I know who my God is, and I have received the greatest miracle of all. Forgiveness."

Nick Vujicic is willing to go on display for all the world to see so that his difficulty can become an impetus for us to proclaim Jesus as he does. His bad; our good.

What are our chains? Our bonds? Are we wasting them with fretting, or are we using them to encourage others to boldness?

Who can we lift up to greater spiritual height today because we are willing to forget ourselves in our trouble and proclaim God's greatness—no matter what?

How Does This Verse Help Me Stand Firm?

How do I see my troubles? Do I see them as personal failures or mini-tragedies in my own soap opera? Perhaps a better way is to see how my handling of my problems can make others take note of God's power to bring peace in the midst of trouble. What a joy it would be to have someone say of me and my difficulty: "I sure learned about God's love because of what you are going through."

What Has to Change?

What is my view of God? Do I think of Him as my personal assistant, here to make my pathway easy? Or do I see Him as the mighty God of the universe whose story I must tell through the things He brings into my life?

PHILIPPIANS 1:15–18

It is true that some preach Christ out of envy and rivalry, but others out of goodwill. The latter do so out of love knowing that I am put here for the defense of the gospel. The former preach Christ out of selfish ambition, not sincerely, supposing that they can stir up trouble for me while I am in chains. But what does it matter? The important thing is that in every way, whether from false motives or true, Christ is preached. And because of this I rejoice.

What You Need To Know

While it was Paul who helped found the church in Philippi, he did not originate the church in Rome. By the time he had arrived in Rome as an itinerate preacher/ missionary who had been arrested, the church had been firmly established in that city.

The church in Rome had begun perhaps eight or nine years before Paul first wrote to the people there in AD 57. In that letter (the book of Romans) he expressed his desire to visit the church in the capital of the empire. Therefore, when Paul arrived, as recorded in Acts 28, perhaps in AD

60 or so, and preached the gospel while in chains, there were already others who were proclaiming the gospel. In fact, when Paul and his fellow travelers finally reached Rome on foot after their nightmarish sea voyage, he was met at a place called Three Taverns by a contingent of Christians (Acts 27–28). From this we can conclude that there were numerous preachers in Rome at the time, and Paul is referring to these men when he speaks of two different kind of preachers—those with good motives and those with questionable ones.

Competitive Preaching

It appears there were two kinds of Christian preachers in Rome—those with pure motives and those who preached to make a name for themselves. Perhaps once the famous Paul came to town, the envious preachers who saw others as rivals were afraid their listeners might prefer the well-known newcomer, so they preached all the harder to make sure that didn't happen.

How that would "stir up trouble" for Paul, we are not sure, but the apostle knew the possibility was there.

Yet here is the surprise. It simply didn't matter.

To Paul, who in another place said, "I have become all things to all people so that by all possible means I might save some" (1 Corinthians 9:22), it was all about the gospel being preached clearly and effectively—without error—so that people could come to a saving knowledge of Christ. And if even the envious preachers were doing that, then "what does it matter"?

This is a rather radical concept for us, isn't it? But remember this: The preachers with the bad motives were out to intimidate or somehow upset Paul, not to preach heresy. And if the only damage done was done to Paul himself, he could take it.

Let's go to church with this idea.

Suppose I have a great idea for a new outreach program. So I spend a lot of time preparing a proposal, and I present it to the evangelism committee. Somehow, and for some mysterious reason (envy, maybe), someone at the committee level turns that idea into his or her own, and it is conveniently forgotten that I dreamed the whole thing up. No one recalls that it was my killer idea. From that point on, the idea is attributed to Committee Member Maggie, or whoever it was. Later, it is implemented and is a success. Maggie gets all the credit while men and women are led to Christ.

Should I sit back and moan about it? Should I be ticked with Maggie? Not for a Pauline minute. "What does it matter," Paul would say. "This is about Jesus, not you." Church is not a competition.

When it came to those who preached the true Word in a way that was not favorable to him, Paul showed godly restraint and mature composure because he realized that spreading the gospel was so much more important than his personal feelings. And the example he sets with his response leads to some searching questions for those of us who want to learn from him.

Is our primary joy seeing Jesus Christ proclaimed, as it was with the jailed apostle? Do we really care who gets the credit when souls are saved and welcomed into the family? Are traditions or personal preferences more important to us than the gospel for which Jesus died?

Let's rejoice, as Paul did, that the gospel is preached.

How Do These Verses Help Me Stand Firm?

It can help me to rethink my attitude toward those who have a heart for ministry but a way of thinking that is different from mine. Young people, for instance, may have a passion for bringing people to Christ but a method that seems a little off the wall to me. Should I thwart their enthusiasm for sharing the gospel just so my preferences are satisfied?

What Has to Change?

Clearly we don't want people preaching the gospel with wrong motives. But that's not the point. What may have to change is my thinking that I have all the answers.

PHILIPPIANS 1:19–20

I know that through your prayers and God's provision of the Spirit of Jesus Christ, what has happened to me will turn out for my deliverance. I eagerly expect and hope that I will in no way be ashamed, but will have sufficient courage so that now as always Christ will be exalted in my body, whether by life or by death.

What You Need to Know

The apostle Paul's trial in Rome did not go well. It went so poorly, in fact, that after two years of having him detained, the Roman government had him executed.

Or not. We're not sure.

We don't really know what happened concerning Paul's imprisonment and impending trial, because the book of Romans doesn't tell us. It could be inferred from the story that Paul did indeed eventually stand trial—based on Acts 27:23–24. After the shipwreck described in that chapter, Paul announced that an angel told him, "Do not be afraid, Paul. You must stand trial before Caesar." If God had that message conveyed to Paul via an angel, it seems likely that proclamation would have been carried out.

Scholars debate the issue of how that trial turned out, but no one knows for sure how it ended. Some say Paul was executed and some say he was acquitted.

Luke, writing under the inspiration of the Holy Spirit, did not let us in on that part of Paul's biography. He simply ended his account of Paul's acts by saying he lived two years in his rented detention home and that he preached the gospel boldly.

So, what you need to know is that we don't know.

Confidence in Uncertainty

Imagine being on Death Row. Knowing that you will never leave prison alive. Knowing that instead of each day promising a bright new hope of happiness and success, it is another dark, dreary advance toward death.

Now imagine a different prison scenario: not knowing whether you are slated for death at the hands of the justice system or you are going to be released to walk the streets a free person again. That was Paul's situation. He knew he could be executed, yet he also knew he might not be.

And here's the thing: Dr. Luke, Paul's traveling companion on the trip to Rome aboard the ship that sank in the aftermath of a wicked storm (Acts 27), leaves us hanging. He ends his record of Paul in Rome without telling us the outcome of Paul's imprisonment. All he tells us is that Paul spent two years under house arrest, but after that—who knows?

While Luke's record leaves us hanging about the outcome, there is one thing we know for sure. According to Paul's letter to the people of Philippi, written during his imprisonment, he had every confidence in God's provision no matter what the outcome.

In a sense, we can relate to Paul. Uncertainty likes to visit us just as it did him when he was in Rome. Think of all the things we cannot know for sure.

I have a friend, a man with a wife and three kids, who went many, many months without a job. Imagine his anxiety when time after time he had to sit before interviewers, spill out his life to them, and impress them with his expertise—only to go home again and wait for the phone to ring.

Over and over, it didn't ring. For many long months.

Then he got a call from a global company that had the perfect position available for his skills. Again, the interviews. The questions. The opportunity to meet his could-be colleagues. Finally, he was told that he had made it into the Top Two.

Then another round of meetings. The waiting. The praying. The uncertainty. And then the phone call. The company decided on the other person.

But my friend didn't turn his back on God and blame Him for yet another turn-down. He accepted the uncertainty and continued to trust. A couple of days later the company called back. Turns out they had another position available, and my friend was perfect for that job. Because of his faithful trust, he could celebrate God's provision.

Oh, yes. I failed to mention this: My friend had just gone through two years of a different kind of uncertainty as he and his wife ushered their elementary-aged daughter through a bout with cancer. That uncertainty had stalked them all this time as well—and this was a matter of life and death—yet they faithfully proclaimed God's goodness throughout.

A new job and a daughter in remission didn't assure them of certainty for the future, but their confidence in God throughout their ordeals assured them of victory no matter what life would throw at them next.

That's Paul's lesson here. He did not know what the Romans were going to do with him. Yet he refused to give in to despair and fear.

Look at the resources Paul had at his disposal as he wore the chains of imprisonment and bore the shackles of uncertainty:

- Prayers from fellow believers (v. 19)
- Help from the Holy Spirit (v. 19)
- Confidence in God's deliverance (v. 19)
- The expectation of shame-free living (v. 20)
- The courage to let Christ be exalted no matter what (v. 20)

These are the resources of the faithful and the building blocks of a foundation of confidence in God and His role in our lives.

Keep this in mind. Those resources were buttressing Paul in a time of uncertainty. They didn't assure him that he would escape the executioner, but they kept him aware of a great truth that can calm the heart of the uncertain Christian: To live is Christ. To die is gain. Either way, victory.

Paul had spiritual resources to shore him up for his daily journey, and he had a God-directed philosophy that took the pressure off the uncertainty.

To live. We like this part, but do we add "is Christ"? Do we wrap up our lives in loving and living for our Savior? That's the first challenge from Paul.

To die. The old joke says, "I'm not afraid of dying. I just don't want to be there when it happens." But reality says we can't avoid it, and Paul's second challenge relates to that. Do we see the gain of being ushered into God's presence when life here is over?

Uncertainty cannot be avoided. But its terror can be reduced if we follow Paul's example. Life is full of uncertainty, but it can't reach our heart if we live with the confidence that comes with being a child of the King.

How Do These Verses Help Me Stand Firm?

It keeps me aware that I am never without resources, even in uncertain times. I have the prayers of the faithful to shore me up and the divine promise of help from the Holy Spirit. I can certainly stand taller and firmer in the face of the winds of trouble with these resources at my disposal.

What Has to Change?

What does uncertainty do to me? Am I living in fear because of job questions or family concerns or physical difficulties? Paul had the hope that "sufficient courage" would lift his spirits so Christ's name would be lifted up. Do I need to exchange frequent anxiety for divine courage?

PHILIPPIANS 1:22–24

If I am to go on living in the body, this will mean fruitful labor for me. Yet what shall I choose? I do not know! I am torn between the two: I desire to depart and be with Christ, which is better by far; but it is more necessary for you that I remain in the body.

What You Need to Know

Some important doctrine can be deduced from these verses. We all want to know what happens to us once we die. Do we go into some suspended state of unconsciousness to await a future awakening with the saints? And if we are conscious, where will we be and what will we see?

"I desire to depart and be with Jesus," Paul writes, pining for a heavenly visit with the Savior. This passage clearly indicates that we will be in Jesus' presence and we will know it. There seems to be no room here for an interlude of sleep or limbo between earth-life in one moment and heaven-life in the next.

Want to Get Away?

At one time there was a humorous advertisement on American TV that showed a person messing up a situation in an embarrassing way, after which the ad voice-over would ask, "Wanna get away?"

We've all been there. We back into another car in the mall parking lot just as the other driver is stepping out of the car. We don't want to face what is coming next—insurance talk, police report, repair hassles. We just want to get away.

Sometimes, Paul tells us, we feel that way about life.

We think about the glories that will follow this life and how much easier things are going to be on the other side. We see the advantages of heaven. Then we think about this life, and we know how much we are loved and wanted here—how there is so much we still need to do.

We kind of want to get away. But on the other hand, we love the idea of staying.

The word for this is *ambivalence*—or as Paul said, "I am torn between the two" (v. 23). As was mentioned earlier, there was a possibility Paul would be executed, but there was also the possibility that he would be released to continue his work.

So, let's look at the pros and cons of each scenario: stay or depart, earth or heaven.

Stay: Fruitful labor (v. 22). It is true. God does not leave us here on earth after we trust Jesus as Savior just so we can take long walks on the beach and watch Turner Classic Movies. He leaves us here so we can bear fruit for Him. There is the fruit of spiritual growth as Paul describes in Galatians 5. There is the fruit of raising children in a family as Psalm 127 describes. There is the fruit of leading others to faith in Christ (Romans 7:4). There is the fruit of good works (Colossians 1:10). All this is the "fruitful labor" that is possible if God allows us to stay around on this earth.

Depart: Be with Christ (v. 23). Isn't that what we all want? After all, Jesus is the name always on our lips. He is the one we love and worship for what He did for us. He is the embodiment of perfection and love. To be in His presence is our lifelong goal. Imagine standing next to the One who was there at creation, who wrestled Jacob, who checked out of heaven's glories to become a Bethlehem baby, who healed, raised, taught, fed, and amazed people throughout Israel. Contemplate the ecstasy of being in His presence!

If Paul had a vote regarding "Which is the more desired outcome—sticking around this big, blue marble or being face-to-face with Jesus in heaven," he has already cast his ballot. Being with Jesus would be "far better."

But only if that is what Jesus wants us to do. The higher priority for us is not to argue which scenario we would prefer but to be satisfied in whichever situation God has called us to live. And for now, He wants us serving Him in the place He has put us. As with Paul, "it is more necessary . . . that [we] remain in the body" (v. 24).

The Pauline challenge is too important to be missed or dismissed. It is too vital for us to ignore it or allow it to slip our notice. "If I am to go on living in the body, this will mean fruitful labor for me" (v. 22).

Think about this idea. Does that sound like me? Am I known as a fruitful Christian? Do people see me as one who spreads

God's love to others? When I am around others, is the fragrance of my presence suggestive of Christlike compassion and kindness?

When it comes to the way we live, we should bask in the reality that God has left us here for His honor, His glory, and so that His name can be praised. And that comes to us and to others only as we practice "fruitful labor."

How Do These Verses Help Me Stand Firm?

It demands that I consider my reason for being here—for breathing God's air and walking His earth. I will stand firmer and more confidently if I day-by-day thank Him for the privilege of seeing the sun come up another day and using my life to reflect the light of Christ's love to others.

What Has to Change?

Do others see me as a joyous occupant of this world? If not, how can I live in a way that says to God, "Thanks for allowing me to be here"?

12

PHILIPPIANS 1:25-26

Convinced of this, I know that I will remain, and I will continue with all of you for your progress and joy in the faith, so that through my being with you again your boasting in Christ Jesus will abound on account of me.

What You Need to Know

As mentioned previously, we do not know if Paul was actually released from his incarceration or was executed by Roman officials. There is some historical precedence for thinking that Paul survived. At least two historians, Clement of Rome and Eusebius, say that Paul left Rome unscathed. Clement said in his account that Paul traveled as far west as Spain.

There also seems to be evidence that Paul wrote some of the epistles after his first stay in Rome and before his second visit. It is possible that during that time he could have revisited Philippi, as he so much wanted to do (1:26).

Eusebius records that Paul was killed in Rome on a return trip—after Nero had burned the city. Legend suggests that Paul was again arrested and that he spent time in the famous Mamertine prison in Rome. Above the entrance of that prison is carved out this phrase: "prison of the saints and apostles Peter and Paul" (PRIGIONE DEI SS APOSTOLI PIETRO E PAOLO).

Well-Placed Confidence

Misplaced confidence can be a dangerous thing. We see this when someone makes a prediction about when the world will end or when Jesus will return. That cannot be a confidence based on godly enlightenment or on a clear reading of Scripture, since the Bible expressly tells us not to make such declarations. That kind of thing happens when someone has a misplaced confidence in a private interpretation of a Bible passage and then arrogantly broadcasts that message to a world too eager to give that person his fifteen minutes of fame (or infamy).

Paul's confidence when he wrote "Convinced of this" wasn't like that. It wasn't some starry-eyed vision based on a bloated sense of self-importance. It was confidence that was God-ordained and perhaps even indicated by the actual situation.

We don't know if Paul had received a favorable word from those in charge of his upcoming trial, but we do know that his words in this passage were God-breathed. No question about it, Paul was confident that he would survive his incarceration and any trial that might follow.

But here's the good part. Look at what Paul does with this confidence. He uses it to encourage the people back in Philippi: "I know that I will remain, and I will continue with all of you for your progress and joy in the faith."

Think about the confidence you have built up in your faith—how you know that God has promised to care for you, meet your needs, teach you about himself, and help you bring glory to His name. Is it possible He is doing that so you can build spiritual growth and "progress," to use Paul's word, into others? And is your faith in action something that can bring "joy," Paul's other word, to those who know you and observe your Christlikeness?

A confident believer in Jesus understands that each new day is given so that God's name can be glorified and His will can be done through our dependence on Him. We show our faith by making sure that others around us are cared for, are encouraged, are challenged in godliness, and are able to see Jesus in us.

As much as is possible, let's confidently lead others to bask in the joy of their salvation and shine in the light of Jesus' love.

How Do These Verses Help Me Stand Firm?

It reminds me that confidence is not cockiness. I am confident because of God, and I can encourage others because of His love and goodness.

What Has to Change?

How do people feel when I enter a room? Do I bring a Christlike joy? Do I at least convey a touch of goodness and godly grace? If not, perhaps I can work to shine my light a bit brighter.

PHILIPPIANS 1:27–28

Whatever happens, conduct yourselves in a manner worthy of the gospel of Christ. Then, whether I come and see you or only hear about you in my absence, I will know that you stand firm in the one Spirit, striving together as one for the faith of the gospel without being frightened in any way by those who oppose you. This is a sign to them that they will be destroyed, but that you will be saved—and that by God.

What You Need To Know

Who is Paul talking about here when he says "those who oppose" the people in Philippi?

Keep in mind that this letter was written to a group of people who knew exactly what Paul was talking about when he talked about the opposition. Therefore, he didn't have to spell out who their opponents were.

One speculation is that some loyal Roman citizens opposed the Christians' reference to Jesus as "Lord." This was a designation Romans reserved for their emperors. Also, there is some thought that the people in the church were facing persecution similar to what Paul seemed to have faced in Ephesus (1 Corinthians 15:32). Whatever the case, it seems there was opposition that was causing concern for the people in the church at Philippi.

Worthy Conduct

Society has changed so much since the 1960s cultural revolution started and took hold, and many in the church have gone right along with it in adopting new philosophies on how to live. Sadly, it is no longer the norm for Christians to have a uniform set of Christ-honoring standards to live by that is acceptable by most believers. Thus we have some people who say they follow Jesus but think nothing of hanging out in bars and drinking the night away with their buddies. Things such as gambling and even sexual activity outside of marriage have become acceptable to many, while college students at Christian universities write papers supporting same-sex marriage and legalization of marijuana.

Such societal-driven standards make it harder and harder to see how Paul's admonition to "conduct yourselves in a manner worthy of the gospel of Christ" (1:27) applies today. Is it even possible to know what "worthy conduct" is?

Interestingly, in this passage it is not a dos and don'ts kind of conduct that Paul is advocating. It is, as some would say, more philosophical. Let's look at the main characteristics of what Paul calls worthy conduct:

- "You stand firm in the one Spirit." Unity. Togetherness. Oneness of purpose. That is what Paul expected of those who populated the Philippian church—and by extension us. Our ability to "stand firm" as a body of believers in Jesus is built on the concept of acting together as one on behalf of the gospel.

Imagine how that could look where we worship. Imagine a group of Christians whose sole purpose is to make sure that the gospel of the Lord Jesus Christ—the story of His death, burial, and resurrection for sin leading to our salvation—remains the centerpiece of all we do.

That's much more important than fighting over whether it's a sin to play touch football on Sunday afternoon or to quibble over which videos we can or cannot watch. A cohesive understanding of God's truth mixed with a collective effort to keep the good news of Jesus at the center of all of our activities is indeed a launching point for worthy conduct.

- "Without being frightened in any way by those who oppose you." Courage. Steadfastness. Bravery in the face of opposition. It seems clear that the Philippians were up against those who did not appreciate this gospel message. How relevant that is to us today! No matter where we turn, it seems, we see those who oppose or despise or do not want to hear the sweet truth of Jesus' offer of salvation. We need Paul's encouragement to stand our ground and to resist the urge to cower before the enemies of grace.

Paul wasn't sure, as has been explained, whether he would ever be able to visit his beloved friends at Philippi. But it really didn't matter if he did or didn't do that. What mattered was that they learned from him—as he remained in his Roman chains–the essence of being a gospel-proclaiming, unified body in this new thing called the church.

What did Paul mean when he talked about worthy conduct? He meant that we should stand together as believers who are sharing the good news with others. And in that unity of purpose, informed by scriptural teaching, we find courage to overcome the fear that could result from reaching out to those who "will be destroyed" if they reject God's truth.

Unity and courage. What a message Paul sent across the miles to the people at Philippi—and what a challenge he has sent across the centuries to us!

How Do These Verses Help Me Stand Firm?

One lonely tree standing against a mighty wind has a greater chance of falling than that same tree surrounded by a forest of protective neighbors. Likewise, unity in the gospel and in the purpose of proclaiming it helps me as a believer to outlast the storms of life. Stand in unity with others, and I will stand firm.

What Has to Change?

If I lack courage, what can change me into a person of strength? It might help to understand that in another of his letters Paul said that we are strong in our weakness (2 Corinthians 12:10). It is not my power that strengthens me, but an acknowledgment of and a dependence on God's power.

PHILIPPIANS 1:29–30

For it has been granted to you on behalf of Christ
not only to believe in him, but also to suffer for him,
since you are going through the same struggle you
saw I had, and now hear that I still have.

What You Need To Know

If we are to trust God and live a life that honors Him, it is essential that we understand His sovereignty—His control. Without that knowledge in our mind and that confidence in our heart, we easily travel down the "woe is me" trail of life. We shuffle along from trouble to trouble, thinking that bad luck or karma or fate is directing our steps. But here Paul is reminding us that what transpires in life—from our belief to our stumbles—"has been granted to you." Our great God directs our lives with love, and He knows what we need, what we can handle, and what will bring praise to Him. An understanding of sovereignty saves us from the despair of randomness and restores our eagerness to do everything for God's glory.

I've Got Bad News . . . and More Bad News

"You've been given the right to suffer just like I'm suffering." Is this any way to encourage people? Seriously.

A guy who is languishing in prison in a country that has brutally conquered the land where you live is sending you a letter that tells you that you too are in a pickle because you trusted him.

It goes something like this: Because you have accepted the message I and others have told you—this story about a Jewish man who was a hero but who was murdered and then surprised everybody by coming back to life—you are in for a hard time.

Paul had just finished challenging the folks in Philippi to tell even more people about this story, this gospel, and not to be afraid when they did it. And now he is telling them: "Uh, did I mention that you are going to suffer because you believed what I told you?" And he even makes it sound like someone is doing them a favor by giving them an opportunity to be persecuted.

Listen to what he says: "It has been granted to you on behalf of Christ not only to believe in him, but also *to suffer for him*, since you are going through the same struggle you saw I had, and now hear that I still have."

This is so foreign to our "believe Jesus and tiptoe through the tulips all the way home to heaven" ears! We are not wired this way as twenty-first-century Christians. But that is because we don't see this the way Paul meant it. We look at what he is saying and think, "Those poor people. What have they gotten themselves into? If only they had known!"

Paul, though, meant it something like this: "Congratulations! You have the privilege of suffering for the sake of the King of

Kings and the Lord of Lords. If you face adversity for the cause of Christ, you are displaying God's grace and reveling in His favor."

There is a huge difference between a *perceived* suffering for the cause and an *actual* suffering for Jesus' sake. The former is the person who trumps up some problem in the church of his own making and then feels sorry for himself when he faces corrective opposition. It's the person who insists the church get purple carpet for the sanctuary and then feels persecuted because everyone else votes for beige.

The latter is the person who genuinely and in a Christlike way attempts to share the good news and the truth of Scripture and is mocked or berated for doing so. Or the person who, in some cultures, gets hauled off to jail for voicing his beliefs.

The first person is suffering for his own sake and is not eligible for God's grace in the situation. The second is an honored soldier of the cross who is serving in a privileged place. He has God's approval and His care.

The Christian faith can seem such a paradox. What seems to be so negative—facing opposition "on behalf of Christ"—is honored and considered a privilege.

The story of a young boy in the Philippines illustrates how this can work. The youngster was raised in a religion that does not recognize Jesus as the Savior. But one day, through the witness of his grandfather, the boy trusted Jesus at the age of eleven. For the next several years he was mocked and derided on a daily basis by his classmates. They called him an infidel and bullied him mercilessly. When he became a young adult, he received biblical training and worked in a discipleship program. Of his past, he said, "When I remember my old friends, my heart breaks. I lost them, and though they turned out to be my enemies, I don't hate them. Instead, I pray for them that they will meet my Lord Jesus and be changed."

As we look around at our situation, are we willing to stand firm for Him when it's not easy? Without looking for trouble by irresponsible behavior, are we ready to risk our safety and comfort on His behalf—to "suffer for Him"?

For over two thousand years, this is how the proclamation of the gospel has kept going, and how lives have been and are being changed. Like everything God does, it works.

How Do These Verses Help Me Stand Firm?

It reminds me that there is a very good reason to stand firm in the face of opposition—and that reason has nothing to do with me. God knew problems would come, He told us about them, but He also provides power and courage and help when they do.

What Has to Change?

Am I willing to take small, beginning steps in sharing the gospel? Am I okay with having to expose my weakness so God's power can be revealed?

PHILIPPIANS 2

HUMILITY, BLAMELESSNESS, AND PERSONAL BUSINESS

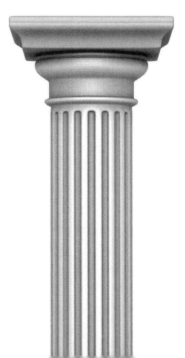

PHILIPPIANS 2:1–2

If you have any encouragement from being united with Christ, if any comfort from his love, if any common sharing in the Spirit, if any tenderness and compassion, then make my joy complete by being like-minded, having the same love, being one in spirit and of one mind.

What You Need To Know

The Beatles claimed that "all you need is love." But, according to Paul, if the folks in Philippi were to accomplish all that the church is called to do, they would need more than love. As Paul writes here, they were to be "united with Christ," and to have "comfort from his love," "common sharing in the Spirit," and "tenderness and compassion."

Apparently it was necessary to spell this out for the church at Philippi—and Paul was making an important appeal to them to change. All they needed was unity, comfort, fellowship, tenderness, and compassion—all things that start with love. Wouldn't Paul's formula here change church life—if it were applied?

Make My Day

Parents love it when their children agree with them. When a child mirrors the thinking of his or her parents, Mom and Dad beam with joy.

"You know what, Dad?" says the eighteen-year-old son. "You know how you always used to tell me that I should stay, like, sexually pure before marriage? Well, me and my girlfriend have decided that's what we're gonna do. We're like, you know, gonna save ourselves for marriage."

With these words, he has made his parents' day with his commitment to purity—something they have spent years trying to lovingly teach their son. Now he says he accepts their teaching and is making it his own. In a sense, he has made his parents' joy complete.

That's the picture Paul is giving us here. He is telling his spiritual sons and daughters that certain Spirit-led actions on their part will make his "joy complete," will make his day. And if, as we examine our lives, we also make a little of this if-then stuff happen to bring honor to our heavenly Father, He will be pleased with us. Our heavenly Father is longing for us to live by the principles spelled out in these verses:

- If your unity with Christ—your salvation—brings encouragement, then make my joy complete.
- If you receive any comfort from Christ's love, then make my joy complete.
- If you have any fellowship with God's Holy Spirit, then make my joy complete.
- If you have observable love for your fellow believer, then make my joy complete.

What a great list! Think of life lived that way.

As an honor to our beloved Savior, we are encouraged, we are comforted, we walk with the Spirit, and we treat our fellow believers well. That in itself would revolutionize the church.

But this remarkable passage doesn't end there! To truly bring Christian unity and make the joy of our brother and sisters complete and honor our Father in heaven, we are spurred by that first list to practice these vital items: like-mindedness, common love, and unity of spirit and purpose with those who share our faith.

Take a moment to imagine a church life where this is our way of operating. Envision for a moment a body of believers meeting together to celebrate these traits.

What if we were to gather in genuine love?

What if we were to celebrate in unity?

What if we were to serve both the church and the community with single-minded purpose?

We would revolutionize our world!

Think about how this works: Our salvation spurs our unity. Our shared Jesus-love brings us comfort in the midst of any trouble. Our collective love for one another helps us overcome differences of preferences, traditions, and agendas.

No wonder this prospect makes Paul's joy complete.

This is the body of Christ as He envisioned it, enabling us to concentrate on God's plan as a unified force.

Go ahead. Make the world's day!

How Do These Verses Help Me Stand Firm?

Is there someone I can encourage by living for Christ? This is often a strong incentive. Just as the Philippians could do all this to make Paul's joy complete, I will think of someone who will benefit by my living as verses 1 and 2 suggest.

What Has to Change?

There is a lot here, so why not just start with one principle. Perhaps I can work on one a week for a month by studying what the Bible says about that first characteristic, and then try to incorporate it in my life.

PHILIPPIANS 2:3–4

Do nothing out of selfish ambition or vain conceit.
Rather in humility value others above yourselves,
not looking to your own interests but each of you
to the interests of others.

What You Need To Know

Remember those preachers in Rome who were presenting the gospel out of selfish ambition (1:17)? The term Paul used to describe them is the same word used here (2:3). Perhaps Paul is repeating this word to remind his friends in Philippi that he does not want them to be motivated by such self-serving attitudes. The apostle then offers a contrast that might help them. Instead of "selfish ambition," he says, try "humility." This may not have been a popular idea back in the day (any more than it is today). Sometimes the term "humility" was used as a negative word that spoke of being a coward. However, something changes when humility is controlled by the Holy Spirit. Then it turns into something extremely positive.

> Only when we practice humility are we able to take the next step, and that is to look at our fellow believers and see their needs, their talents, their interests, and allow them full service in the kingdom. This is what it means to avoid selfish ambition. If we forget ourselves for a while and allow the hopes, dreams, and service of others to flourish, the church benefits.

Is It Really "All about me"?

Let's start with the story of the two-tone roof.

As the tale is told, it was time for the church to get a new set of shingles to keep the rain out. So a committee was appointed to discuss this repair, and they decided to fund the re-roofing of the church building. That's when things got interesting. And a bit weird.

The committee was split on the all-important question of what color shingles to buy. One group wanted to get green shingles. The other group favored red. Negotiations, arguments, and stubbornness followed. When the dust cleared and it was time to settle on a color, neither side would budge.

So, in a compromise that would clearly tell the community that this group of Christians just couldn't get along, the church opted for a half green, half red roof.

At least it looked good at Christmastime.

Paul would not have liked this roof. Paul favored unity, love, and like-mindedness. This roof was the color of disunity, dislike, and contention.

When Paul brings up "selfish ambition" in verse three, it's the second time he has used this term. As mentioned above, the first was in 1:17 when he discussed the preachers who were energized by "selfish ambition" to spread the gospel.

Remember how that went? Paul actually gave in a bit to the "selfish ambition" crowd in that context because, in the mystery of God's grace, even with selfishness in their hearts, those preachers were commended. But that situation was more about the importance of the gospel than about how we are to do things. Jesus' name must be proclaimed and His salvation must be broadcast. So much was riding on the supreme importance of the message that God allowed for a bad messenger.

But here, in chapter 2, something different is going on. Paul is about to use Jesus himself as an example of the attitude and actions we should have, so he says boldly, "Do nothing out of selfish ambition or vain conceit."

There is a wonderful irony going on in this passage. While the emphasis is on setting aside selfishness and vanity, Paul balances his teaching with some helpful and delicious reality. When Paul says that we "should look not only to [our] own interests," he is acknowledging that when we are working with other believers, we do bring something to the table. We are not to completely set aside our feelings, our findings, our knowledge in a situation. Yet our interests must be tempered with the interests of others. We don't have to give in to others in every case, he seems to be saying, but we must at least give them equal consideration.

Having been around churches my whole life, I think I know how this can go awry. For instance, let's say a person—let's call him George—who has for a long time appreciated and supported his pastor—gradually becomes disenchanted with him for reasons that relate to preference in teaching and leadership methods and not doctrine or heresy. George begins to feel uncomfortable sitting under this pastor's leadership. In other words, when he looks after his own interests, he feels that it is time for the pastor to move on.

What often happens in a case like this is that George, because of selfish ambition or vain conceit or some other reason, wants to make sure his interests are reflected in others. So, instead of quietly leaving and going to another church, continuing to pray for the pastor, and supporting him to others, he stays and begins undercutting the pastor with his comments. Soon, a rift appears in the church, and the work of a pastor who is serving God faithfully is interrupted.

George has forgotten that the interests of others—the ones who enjoy the pastor's leadership—need to be looked out for as well as his own. Instead of protecting their interests, he has allowed self-centeredness to make him think his interests have to be everyone else's.

Let's turn Paul's admonitions around. Let's do everything with selfless concern instead of selfish ambition. Let's serve our Savior with humble confidence in Him. And let's give equal consideration to the concerns of our fellow believers.

Imagine how our testimony would shine to all who watch us if we were to do that! Imagine what would have happened if someone had begun negotiations for a new roof by reading Philippians 2:3. Perhaps a nice brown roof would have graced that edifice—and the community would have seen what unity looks like.

How Do These Verses Help Me Stand Firm?

It focuses concern where it belongs—on the work of God in the church. And it reduces the focus on what doesn't matter as much—my personal preference.

What Has to Change?

Is my first thought always, "What do I think about this?" Or is my first thought, "What can I do to help the cause of Christ in this situation?" How often do I look at the concerns of others as much as I look at my own?

PHILIPPIANS 2:5

Have the same mindset as Christ Jesus.

What You Need to Know

Paul never met Jesus face to face. In that regard, he was very much like us. However, he had an advantage that we don't have—he knew those who had actually walked and talked with Jesus. Peter, for one. When he and Paul were together, they must have spoken of the Savior. And Luke, while he never knew Jesus personally, was such a great researcher and historian that surely he conveyed what he knew to Paul.

So, what is the point of this? The point is that while we have never met the Savior in person (not even as Paul did on the road to Damascus), we can know what His attitude was—the attitude we are to emulate. And even if we have never thought about this question before, we can learn about Jesus' attitude as Paul explains it to us in verses 6–11. Combine that with what we already know about the Savior from the writings of Matthew, Mark, Luke, and John, and we have no excuse for not being aware enough of Jesus' attitude to mirror it.

Attitude Adjustment

Who is the most Jesus-like person you have ever heard about—outside of people in the Bible? Is there anyone you've read about or been told about who mirrors Jesus enough that someone might say, "That person has the same attitude as Jesus Christ"? Or perhaps someone you know personally?

Thinking about this might lead some to wonder: What does it mean when Paul says our mindset should be the same as that of Christ Jesus? To help focus in on this, think in these terms: What was important to our Savior as He went about His earthly ministry? What was His attitude . . .

Toward sin?

He cried about it.

Toward sinners?

He hung out with them and loved them despite what others said about His doing so.

Toward religious people?

He hated their hypocrisy and the ignorance they showed toward Scripture.

Toward women?

He showed an anti-cultural respect for them and a willingness to forgive the fallen. And think of how while suffering on the cruel cross He thought of his mother.

Toward children?

He had time for them and showed gentle love to them.

Toward the broken?

He healed them and spent time with them.

Toward Scripture?

He honored it, quoted it, and authenticated it.

What do we see in action in Jesus' life? We see compassion, selflessness, love, respect, authenticity, and honor. And what kind of attitude leads to those kinds of actions? It all begins with humility.

A nineteenth-century poet named Amiel clarified how this works: "There is no respect for others without humility in one's self." The key to our Savior's interaction with others after He began His public ministry of preaching and healing and caring for the troubled was His humility (more about this in verses 6–8).

Clearly, we are not living in the age of humility. Everywhere we look we see pride and arrogance. We see power grabs and put-downs. We see strutting and upstaging as people battle for the spotlight.

Imagine the contrast we can bring to our world if we have Jesus' attitude. Think of how humbling ourselves to help others will attract people to our message. Consider how putting others before ourselves will win respect and gain a hearing as we try to tell them about our Jesus.

Just as Paul desired that the people of Philippi would capture the spirit of Jesus' humility in their assembly of believers, so we too should seek that same attitude in our lives—both inside and outside of the church.

How Does This Verse Help Me Stand Firm?

Jesus was indeed our example, and short of His miracles and His redemptive sacrifice, I should seek to emulate His attitude in my life. Standing firm takes Christlike humility, Christlike compassion, Christlike love, Christlike unselfishness, and Christlike trust in God. Surely a little more of those things will strengthen me.

What Has to Change?

Do I need an attitude check? What have I done lately that makes me look at all like Jesus? Can I start with one Christlike attitude and, with His help, try to follow that in my life?

PHILIPPIANS 2:6–7

[Jesus], being in very nature God, did not consider equality with God something to be used to his own advantage; rather he made himself nothing, by taking the very nature of a servant, being made in human likeness.

What You Need to Know

Have you ever really thought about what Jesus gave up for us when He left heaven to come to earth? Just in practical, down-to-earth terms? Take, for instance, this short statement made about Him: "The Son of Man has no place to lay his head" (Matthew 8:20, Luke 9:58). It's pretty clear that once He began His ministry after leaving his boyhood home, Jesus had no home. For example, when He went to Capernaum for a time He stayed with friends. Do you know anyone who is currently "staying with friends"? That usually means a lack of funds, a humble situation, and a touch of embarrassment. In earthly terms, Jesus was homeless.

Contrast that with what He left behind: the boundless riches of heaven. In 2 Corinthians 8:9, Paul wrote,

> "Though he was rich, yet for your sake he became poor, so that you through his poverty might become rich."

Christmas: The Prequel

When Christmas rolls around each year and we begin to think of the best passage of Scripture to use to tell the story of the baby Jesus, we usually land in the early pages of Matthew or Luke. But have you ever thought of starting here—with Philippians 2:6–7?

On the surface it may not seem to fit because there are no angels or shepherds or wise men hovering about with their gifts. No stars. No feeding trough. No swaddling clothes. Indeed, Mary and Joseph don't even make a cameo appearance. So it might not seem very Christmas-y.

However, this passage is what Christmas is all about. It's a little like a prequel in a novel or a movie—giving us the backstory of what happened to the main character before we first meet him or her. In these verses Paul gives us a sneak-peek into the thought processes of our Savior before He made His surprising appearance on that silent night in Bethlehem.

Throughout a timeless past, the triune Godhead existed together—the Father, the Son, and the Holy Spirit. They shared equally in their God-ness, a mysterious idea that we know next to nothing about—and which in many ways is beyond our human understanding. Then, at a point that we call "in the beginning," they cast the vast and seemingly limitless universe out into what had been endless nothingness. And not much later, the human creations bearing their image—the ones into whom they breathed life to signal the start of the human race—decided to rebel, and a promise was given to those humans that a Redeemer would one day visit them (Genesis 3:15).

That Redeemer, the Godhead knew, would be the Son—the one we call Jesus.

But for that to happen, an unimaginable thing would have to take place. That promised Savior, who was "in very nature God" and who had been so for all eternity, would have to step out of the majestic glories of heaven and descend to the sin-pocked world called earth. After an eternal fellowship of perfection in an existence of magnificence and splendor, Jesus would have to take the biggest demotion ever known.

Willingly letting go of what He deserved because of His divine nature—constant heavenly co-existence with the Father and the Spirit—Jesus "made himself nothing." Not for a moment letting go of His deity (He was, after all, Emmanuel, "God with us," Matthew 1:23), Jesus let go of His rightful benefits to become the most helpless of beings—a human baby. The Creator of the universe (Hebrews 1:2) became Mary's little lamb. He endured the humility and helplessness of being an infant.

But there is even more. Before Jesus became that helpless little baby, He knew that His life on earth would be marked by a trait that is not usually associated with deity. He would become a servant. "Very nature God" became "very nature servant." He came not to be served, but to serve, as Mark so clearly explains (10:45).

Knowing the rest of the story should help us as we set up the nativity scene next Christmas. No longer will we think just of the baby in the manger. Now we will think as well about the heavenly scene that preceded it as Jesus contemplated His selfless decision to make himself nothing for us.

How Do These Verses Help Me Stand Firm?

If this concept does nothing else, it certainly should shake up any unmerited ego I might have. The contrast between the greatness of God and my puniness is gargantuan. Jesus set aside His glories; I seem to always be looking to gain new ones. That's why I need that attitude adjustment I learned about in verse 5.

What Has to Change?

How do I think of Jesus? Do I always see Him in His human state hanging out with Matthew and Peter? Or do I think about His untold glories in heaven and contemplate what it might have been like to set them aside?

PHILIPPIANS 2:8

And being found in appearance as a man,
he humbled himself by becoming obedient
to death—even death on a cross!

What You Need To Know

While verse 8 reiterates a truth found in verse 7—
that Jesus was made in human likeness and was therefore
"found in appearance as a man"—it also provides us with
a startling reminder of what Jesus set aside to become our
Savior. The verse states, "He humbled himself by becoming obedient to death—even death on a cross!" This is a
depth of humility that cannot be overstated.

When we look back at Isaiah 53, we realize how Jesus'
humility took away every shred of human decency: "He
had no beauty or majesty to attract us to him, nothing in
his appearance that we should desire him" (53:2). Unbe-
lievable. Here was the glorious Savior, the Son of the living God who shared the heavenly majesty and glory. Yet
in His humility that was all taken away. But look at what
the prophet said next: "He was despised and rejected by

mankind, a man of suffering and familiar with pain" (53:3). And all of this was before the cross. And, of course, it grows worse. Verse 5 tells us, "He was pierced for our transgressions, he was crushed for our iniquities." And finally, Deuteronomy 21:23 says this: "Anyone who is hung on a pole is under God's curse." Think long and deeply about Philippians 2:8 and what it tells us about our Savior's love for us.

Death Did Not Become Him

Have you ever watched one of those television documentaries that show young teens being taken into a prison to experience what it is like? The goal of the exercise is to help the kids get "scared straight." The idea is that if they go from their life of school and activities that are relatively easy and free of trouble and then are thrust into a prison environment with lots of yelling and hatred and anger and violence, they will think twice about doing something that will get them sentenced to such a place.

Taking relatively innocent kids and subjecting them to the reality of a prison can give us a tiny glimpse of what Jesus might have experienced when He left the innocence of heaven and came to a world full of sin and death. When He willingly became flesh and dwelt among us, Jesus suddenly was living with the consequences of the sins of everyone He encountered—actually, the sins of all humanity, past, present, and future.

And it affected Him.

The results of sin made Him cry.

Greed bothered Him so much He overturned the temple tables.

And death, of course, affected Him most of all.

Death never visited more agony on anyone than it visited on Jesus.

How Does This Verse Help Me Stand Firm?

This passage reminds me of the lengths Jesus went through on my behalf. If I can't stand firm and strong for the One who would do so much for me, it's hard to imagine what I would stand up for.

What Has to Change?

Have I given Christ's great sacrifice much thought? How remarkable and difficult it was! Perhaps rethinking Jesus' troubling, gruesome sacrifice can help me refocus on Him instead of worrying about the trivia that sometimes inundates my life.

PHILIPPIANS 2:9–11

*Therefore God exalted him to the highest place and
gave him the name that is above every name, that at the
name of Jesus every knee should bow, in heaven and on
earth and under the earth, and every tongue acknowledge
that Jesus Christ is Lord, to the glory of God the Father.*

What You Need To Know

In verses 6–8, Paul shines a spotlight on Jesus and
His attitude as he spells out a multi-faceted description
of the humility of the Savior and His willingness to face
death on our behalf. But in verse 9 something new and
different is taking place. The Father God is in the spotlight, and we see how He responds to His Son's action.
In verses 6–8 Jesus is the subject of all the verbs: Jesus
"did not consider," Jesus "made himself nothing," Jesus
"humbled himself." In verse 10, God is the subject and
Jesus becomes the object of His actions.

And what is God's major action? Exaltation. Bible
teacher William Hendriksen calls it a "super-exaltation."

As a result of Jesus' humiliation and willingness to set aside His glory for an earthly journey to the cross, the Father "exalted" the ascended Savior "to the highest place." Furthermore, God bestows on Jesus an outcome that shows how high that place is—in words that harken back to Isaiah 45:23–24, which says of Yahweh himself, "Before me every knee will bow; by me every tongue will swear. They will say of me, 'In the LORD alone are deliverance and strength.' "

In this "highest place," and with the prospect of one day sharing the adulation of the nations that goes to God alone, Jesus is honored by the Father.

The Underdog Wins; We Cheer

Don't you just love those stories where the unlovely child becomes the princess or where the struggling substitute on the basketball team wins the state championship with a surprise three-pointer! We love the underdog, the one who struggles at the beginning but then overcomes all odds to wear the tiara or hold the trophy at the end. Who hasn't shed a tear or two after watching or reading one of those stories?

Listen to the description of the character in this story. Although He came from a rich background and had powers never before possessed by any other little boy, He was born to a poor family in a small village. One description of this baby was that He was "nothing." One report said He had "no beauty or majesty" to attract others to Him. He was called a servant. He was humble. And there is no record of His childhood, except for the time He scared His parents by wandering off and talking to strangers while the family was on a religious pilgrimage.

While He experienced a short season of fame as an adult when He did some things no one else could do, He was hated by the authorities and continually harassed as they tried to trick Him into making a fatal mistake. In fact, by using one of His closest friends to betray Him, they finally tracked him down, held a mock trial, and sentenced Him to torture and death. He was then buried in a borrowed tomb.

But has a sad underdog story ever turned out so good? This Man's death was not the end; it was the beginning. He escaped that borrowed tomb by coming back to life, which secured for us the possibility of a forever life in the place of glory this Man left in order to save us.

And for this Man—this Jesus—there was a total reversal of the humility and trouble and trial that He willingly endured for us.

In these three verses Paul concisely spelled that out for the people of Philippi as a way of telling them that they were worshiping the right Savior, for God exalted Him and lifted Him back to His proper place of adoration.

- His name, Jesus, is the name that stands above all others.
- At the mention of that name, everyone will one day bow a knee.
- Every tongue will eventually cry out praises to this Person to whom so much tragedy occurred during His visit to this planet.

What a story! What a Savior!

In awe we consider how blessed we are that He loves us and has redeemed us. In adulation we speak of His greatness and His salvation. In love we worship Him and thank Him for His incarnation, His life, and His salvation.

How Do These Verses Help Me Stand Firm?

There is nothing like being in on good news before someone else. As a believer in Jesus, I have already begun to give Jesus the praise He deserves—and will get forever in eternity. The more I practice the eternal praise of my Savior, the firmer I will stand for as long as I live on this earth.

What Has to Change?

Do I like to praise the Lord? Is that one area of my life that needs a boost? Whether in song, in prayer, or just in quiet reflection, I will let my soul be touched by Christ's sacrifice and will let my heart lift in greater praise.

PHILIPPIANS 2:12–13

Therefore, my dear friends, as you have always obeyed—
not only in my presence, but now much more in my
absence—continue to work out your salvation with
fear and trembling, for it is God who works in you
to will and to act to fulfill his good purpose.

What You Need To Know

When was Paul present with the people of Philippi? When he says "in my presence," he is likely referring to the events recorded in Acts 16 when Paul and his missionary group, including Luke, visited Philippi. On a Sabbath he visited with a group of Jewish people near a river outside the city. There a businesswoman named Lydia was worshiping with her friends. She listened to the gospel that day and trusted Jesus as Savior. She was the first of many who gathered in her house to worship, which was the beginning of the church in that city.

Paul's work in Philippi also included an episode that got him arrested. He cast demonic spirits out of a girl, and that upset those who had been making money off her troubles. When an earthquake opened the prison doors for Paul to escape, he didn't leave until he had explained the gospel to the jailer. He and his family, we can presume, were part of this church in its early days. These events marked the time when Paul's "presence" was in Philippi and the church got its start.

See How This Works?

Nothing in the world of education is as awkward as the situation a substitute teacher is called upon to endure. Having never been a substitute teacher, my knowledge of this comes from reports I have received after I have left a class in someone else's hands for a day. "Wow! They really don't listen." Or, "What a talkative bunch!" are reports I've received from subs who took my class.

It seems that when the teacher is away, the students will play . . . by a different set of rules.

As Paul wrote these verses to the Philippians (2:12–13), as we well know, the teacher was away. Paul, who had helped begin the church when Lydia and later the Roman jailer and his family were converted, had been able to stay only briefly in Philippi. During that time, he taught the people, and he may have left someone behind (possibly Luke) to continue their instruction. Clearly, he had also left his heart in Philippi.

And now, in this passage, he appeals to them to continue their spiritual growth even though he cannot be there. It's a little like the classroom teacher saying, "I won't be here tomorrow, but I want you to study hard anyway."

But what was the lesson?

It was simply this: Just as you saw the obedience of Jesus and the reward that God bestowed upon Him, I challenge you to obey. I challenge you to "work out your salvation with fear and trembling."

Paul is talking to people who have already experienced the salvation that comes through faith in Jesus Christ. He's not asking them to work for their salvation, for that is contradictory to the clear teaching of the gospel. What he is suggesting, as he made clear in his majestic example of Jesus, is obedience. Paul the teacher is saying, in effect, "See how this works? See what Jesus did? He obeyed" (v. 8).

It also appears that Lydia and others in the church lived in obedience after Paul left because he commends them with these words "as you have always obeyed." And now he is asking more of them. As they stand in awe of God's salvation ("fear and trembling"), they are to display, practice, and model the salvation they had been given. And as that happens, God's will and His "good purpose" will flow.

Paul could not be there to monitor the Christians at Philippi. And our Savior is not standing in front of us physically to "work out our salvation." Yet we have no excuse for not doing God's work on earth. It all comes down to obedience.

How Do These Verses Help Me Stand Firm?

It gives me a picture of what I am to do. I am to obey no matter who is or isn't around. And even then, the results are not up to me; they are up to God, "who works in [me]."

What Has to Change?

I think of this saying: "Your character is what you do when no one is looking." My "no one is around so it doesn't matter what I do" is no excuse. Obedience is always the thing to do.

PHILIPPIANS 2:14–16

Do everything without grumbling or arguing, so that you may become blameless and pure, "children of God without fault in a warped and crooked generation. Then you will shine among them like stars in the sky as you hold firmly to the word of life. And then I will be able to boast on the day of Christ that I did not run or labor in vain.

What You Need To Know

Most scholars who study this passage suggest that when Paul chose the words "grumbling or arguing" (under the guidance of the Holy Spirit, of course) he was purposely recalling for his readers the context of the children of Israel. Surely the first-century folks would have been familiar with this story. Indeed, as was established earlier, the first Christians in Philippi, and perhaps others, had a Jewish background. The famous grumbling of the people in the desert would have been a common tale told in their homes. The difference, it would appear, is that while the children of Israel complained and griped because of things they thought God should have done for them, the people of Philippi seemed to have personal conflicts among themselves. In any case, we can learn from Paul's words that complaining works against the attitudes and actions God expects of us if we intend to "shine like stars."

Star Shine

How did Paul know? How did he know what life would be like in the twenty-first century? When he penned the words "a warped and crooked generation" (v. 14), he could have been describing the world in which we live.

Don't we often think that the era we are living in is the most corrupt and sinful imaginable? We sometimes have the impression that in years gone by things were sparkly clean and free of the terrible sin and degradation of today. *Those were the days, my friend!* Paul's words make me wonder if the people back in his day might have felt the same way. I can just imagine the folks of Philippi saying, "Remember how things were back in the year 10? Yessir, those were the good old days. And now look, we get this letter from Paul, and he's right: This is a warped and crooked generation."

In reality, though, we sometimes see earlier eras through rose-colored glasses. Indeed, the world has always been in such a state that the apostle's description was as accurate in 10 as it was in 310 as it was in 1910 as it is today. Around us is a society that—like societies before—has rejected the Savior and has accepted ungodliness as a welcome norm. It was to this kind of world that Paul gave his advice in verses 14 through 16.

In our world today, do we sometimes hear a bit of "grumbling and arguing"? Of course we do. Just read the commentary section of any article posted on the Internet, and you'll think the world is fifteen minutes away from annihilation. Listen to people discuss politics. Eavesdrop on conversations people have about their families. If there wasn't any grumbling and arguing going on, there would hardly be any conversations at all.

This has been going on for thousands of years. If you have studied the exodus of Israel from Egypt, you know that the desert wanderers under Moses' leadership made a lifelong hobby of griping. They complained about the manna. They complained about not having the leeks and onions of Egypt. They complained about not having enough water. They complained when Moses took too long hanging out with God. Their list of complaints goes on and on.

And it just might be that this is a reference point for Paul as he discusses the need for the Philippian people to avoid "grumbling and arguing." As Paul presents his case for not griping, what he says about it is surprising—and extremely informative. He suggests that this is about more than peaceful coexistence. It is a moral issue. It is about becoming "pure and blameless." Those who avoid grumbling and arguing are "children of God without fault." They shine "like stars in the sky" and proclaim the gospel—the "word of life."

This should jar our world a little. We often consider a little gripe fest here or there as no big deal. We don't mind a good verbal battle once in a while over some pet issue. But Paul puts this in a new light when he calls on the saints in Philippi to stop murmuring about God's dealings with them and to avoid disputes among His people.

A world that has surrendered itself to immorality and godlessness cannot notice us if we are no different from it. Yet think of how we can shine the light of God's love on that crooked world if we trust Him without complaint and love each other enough not to give in to contentions among ourselves. Think of how good a pure and blameless body of Christians will look by contrast.

What Paul is asking is not easy, but it is part of the growing sanctification that should mark our lives as we allow God to work in us "to will and to act in order to fulfill his good purpose" (v. 13).

How Do These Verses Help Me Stand Firm?

It calls me out on my attitude toward others. Perhaps I'm pretty smug about things being my way or the highway. If I take Paul's admonition here seriously, though, I realize that interacting with others God's way is the right way. Anything else blocks me from being star-shine to a world darkened by sin.

What Has to Change?

Perhaps I can begin to keep tabs on the things I murmur and complain about—maybe in a journal. Then, as I review them I can set a goal to eliminate my favorite gripes one at a time. If my attitude changes to one of devotion to God and His glory, then my gripey attitude will change as well.

PHILIPPIANS 2:17–18

*But even if I am being poured out like a drink offering
on the sacrifice and service coming from your faith,
I am glad and rejoice with all of you. So you too
should be glad and rejoice with me.*

What You Need To Know

Paul refers here to a rather minor ritual mentioned in several Old Testament books. In Exodus, during the consecration ceremony for the priests, a lamb was to be offered as a sacrifice. In the procedure a mixture that included flour and olive oil was to be offered as "a drink offering." This was said to create "a pleasing aroma" when it was offered to the Lord by fire (Exodus 29:38–41). A similar drink offering was made by the Israelites soon after entering the Promised Land (Leviticus 23:13). Numbers 6 mentions drink offerings in regard to Nazarite vows, and Numbers 28 explains the drink offering in association with Mount Sinai. The earliest reference to a drink offering is found in Genesis when Jacob offered one at Bethel.

Give It Up for Paul

Why do people give up a day of work, go downtown, and stand in the cold or in the heat (depending on the season) to cheer for athletes who have won a major championship and then parade their way through the city? Have those athletes not been rewarded enough already? They were paid well to play the games throughout the season. They will get grand and expensive rings to wear (or put in a safe deposit box). And they will even get a nice hefty check for winning the championship.

Yet despite all those advantages, fans gladly make an extra effort to show up, shower the athletes with confetti, and rejoice with them as they parade down Main Street.

The fans give it up for their favorite team.

Paul would like that kind of attitude. In fact, that's a little like what he asked for from the folks at Philippi. No, he didn't ask for a parade or the key to the city, but he did want them to "be glad and rejoice" with him. Give it up for Paul, Philippi!

The analogy of fan and athlete stops at this point, though, because in the case of Paul and the Philippians, they were actually teammates. They were part of the same team—the team of shared faith in Jesus Christ.

Paul, living under house arrest far away in Rome, said he was "being poured out like a drink offering" in the sense that he was sacrificing his life for the gospel. He had already given up so much to proclaim the good news far and wide, and at the time of the writing of this letter, as was mentioned earlier, his life was in danger because of those efforts.

Likewise, he was asking the folks in Philippi to make their own kinds of sacrifices for the gospel. And it appears that he assumed they were carrying through on that mission, for he said he was glad and rejoicing with them. He was giving it up for them in verse 17 before asking them to give it up for him in verse 18.

This is pretty radical stuff! Paul is asking—is expecting—his brothers and sisters in Christ to be willing to live a life of sacrifice—as he clearly was doing. It's a call for sacrifice and service in a hostile environment.

It's a challenge not unlike the one accepted by our men and women in the military. They sign up knowing that they will face difficulties and sacrifice, and they develop an *esprit de corps* that aligns with Paul's idea of mutual rejoicing. For example, Marines respect other Marines because they know the trials and tribulations they each have gone through to be able to wear the uniform.

Do we see the Christian life that way? Are we willing to be "poured out like a drink offering" if that is what it takes to fulfill God's will in our lives and to accomplish His purposes?

Give it up for Paul for his sacrifice, and then let's think about what it will take for us give it up each day to create our own life of service for the Lord.

How Do These Verses Help Me Stand Firm?

It reminds me of two words that have gone out of favor today: service and sacrifice. It challenges me to look for ways to serve in Jesus' name and if necessary be willing to sacrifice for the One who sacrificed so much for me.

What Has to Change?

How excited am I for the success of my fellow believers? Do I rejoice with them? To be an offering for the lives of others, I must think of them first and of me second.

PHILIPPIANS 2:19–30

I hope in the Lord Jesus to send Timothy to you soon, that I also may be cheered when I receive news about you. I have no one else like him, who will show genuine concern for your welfare. For everyone looks out for their own interests, not those of Jesus Christ. But you know that Timothy has proved himself, because as a son with his father he has served with me in the work of the gospel. I hope, therefore, to send him as soon as I see how things go with me. And I am confident in the Lord that I myself will come soon.

But I think it necessary to send back to you Epaphroditus, my brother, co-worker and fellow soldier, who is also your messenger, whom you sent to take care of my needs. For he longs for all of you and is distressed because you heard he was ill. Indeed he was ill, and almost died. But God had mercy on him, and not on him only but also on me, to spare me sorrow upon sorrow. Therefore I am all the more eager to send him, so that when you see him again you may be glad and I may have less anxiety. So then, welcome him in the Lord with great joy, and honor people like him, because he almost died for the work of Christ. He risked his life to make up for the help you yourselves could not give me.

What You Need to Know

We cannot begin to understand the sacrifice it was for Epaphroditus to be the messenger of the Philippian people to Paul in Rome. We do know one thing: Epaphroditus risked his life in the process. He somehow became ill, and that illness nearly cost him his life. And now, in this letter, we see the admiration that both Paul and the church have for this man. Paul appreciates Epaphroditus tremendously because of what he has done for him—bringing him a thoughtful gift from the people to minister to Paul's needs. And the people are eagerly awaiting his triumphant return from this long and sometimes life-threatening trip.

Paul spends some time in his letter telling how special his messenger friend is to him. He calls him "my brother," which we well know as a signal of camaraderie and mutual faith among believers. He calls him his "fellow worker," which elevates Epaphroditus to the level of the great missionary's own responsibility of spreading the gospel. And he calls him a "fellow soldier." Both Paul in Rome and the people back home in Roman-occupied Philippi knew all about the value of soldiers. Finally, he designates Epaphroditus as a "messenger." This carries the weight and meaning of the word "apostle," which again elevates Epaphroditus's status. Surely this encouraging letter sent the messenger home with a light heart and a spring in his step.

Family Talk

Do you get prayer letters from your missionary friends? If you're like me, whether they arrive via e-mail or regular mail, you can't wait to open them and get caught up on the news. You are encouraged and challenged by these letters. They tell about victories and defeats, happy times and sad. But most of all they tell you how God is working in a place where you cannot be. These missionary friends are ambassadors on behalf of all of us who care for them.

Think of Philippians 2:19–30 as the prayer letter to end all prayer letters.

Paul is on the hearts of the people of this small church he helped start. They are praying for him. They probably still talk about him often. And they have made both financial and personal investments in him by sending money to Paul and by sending one of their own, Epaphroditus, to make the long journey to Rome to visit the missionary. Now Paul is about to share from his heart about both Epaphroditus and his spiritual son Timothy— two stories that must have warmed the hearts of the church folks when the letter arrived.

Paul knows that the church needs a mentor to help them navigate through some issues. And who better to send than trustworthy Timothy to try to address any areas of disunity that may have cropped up in the church.

Epaphroditus, on the other hand, is being sent as an encouragement. As he was to Paul, he will also be to the people when he returns. Sure, they will be glad to see Timothy for the help he can offer. But Epaphroditus is a returning missionary. Surely a potluck awaits.

How encouraging it is to hear about Paul's plans to send them spiritual help and emotional encouragement—something the Philippians need. Something we all need.

Paul's "missionary letter" reminds us of the value in our own lives of those who are trained and equipped to assist us in understanding God's Word. We need the Timothys of the world to point out areas of weakness and how to overcome them. We need the prophetic input of godly instructors to open our hearts to concepts that make our own lives more godly or more effective. And we need to be encouraged by the Epaphroditus kind of people, just as we need to be that kind of encourager to others.

After we read this part of Paul's letter, we can put it down, sit back, and praise God for the many ways our brothers and sisters, our fellow soldiers, and our messengers can lift us up, inform us, and guide us toward Christlikeness. What a team Paul was creating for his friends in Philippi. Let's make sure we have that kind of team in our own churches as we do the work of the kingdom.

How Do These Verses Help Me Stand Firm?

For one thing, it helps me appreciate fellow believers who are serving far away. And for another, it reminds me that each of us needs both knowledge and encouragement if the entire church is to stand firmer, stronger, and more resolute in fulfilling God's purposes.

What Has to Change?

How do I view those who speak truth and wisdom into my life or into my church's life? Am I eager or reluctant to be taught? The answer will dictate what has to change in my life.

PHILIPPIANS 3

FOR CHRIST, WE PRESS ON

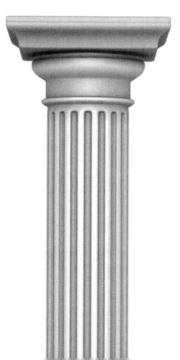

PHILIPPIANS 3:1–3

Further, my brothers and sisters, rejoice in the Lord!
It is no trouble for me to write the same things to you
again, and it is a safeguard for you. Watch out for
those dogs, those evildoers, those mutilators of the flesh.
For it is we who are the circumcision, we who serve
God by his Spirit, who boast in Christ Jesus,
and who put no confidence in the flesh.

What You Need To Know

Paul sounds upset. And he minces no words. Apparently a group of people in Philippi was spreading heresy. These people, who were called Judaizers, declared that faith in Christ alone was not sufficient for salvation. Paul had so much distaste for these heretics that he called them "dogs"—a word that he as a Jew knew was abhorrent to them. Dogs were seen as unclean—and these were not lapdogs Paul was referring to. These dogs were street animals, mongrels—eating whatever garbage they could find and attacking people viciously. Paul used this strong

> language to alert his friends at Philippi to the imminent
> danger these Judaizers posed to the church.

Not to Change the Subject, But . . .

You know how it feels when the pastor reaches a point in his Sunday morning message where he gives you hints that he is about to "land the plane"? He says, "In conclusion," but you've been around long enough to know that he's just circling the airport. He's really not ready to bring it in for a landing.

It's a little like that with Paul as he writes, "Further, my brothers" at this point in his letter (3:1). We can see that there is far too much going on to think that he is shutting things down. (By the way, scholars argue about things like this—wondering if perhaps this section was inserted into the letter later and was not a part of the original.)

But regardless of what is happening with the "further" here, we do know that Paul is about to address something that is far different from his warm and encouraging ending to what we refer to as chapter 2. Paul is about to deal frankly and forcefully with an important issue facing the church.

This is not a new issue, though, for he says, "It is no trouble to write the same things to you *again*." Obviously Paul has discussed this with them before, and he begins with a strong warning: "Watch out for those dogs, those evildoers, those mutilators of the flesh." Harsh words indeed from the great missionary, but they reveal the fear he has in his heart for his people. It is the urgency of a pastor calling on the people of the church to heed truth.

The problem was a group called the Judaizers, who were teaching false doctrine. They were suggesting that the gospel of Jesus' death, burial, and resurrection was not enough for salvation; believers had to be circumcised to be fully saved.

Paul reminds his friends—and us by the long extension of history—of the rock-solid basis of a faith we can stand on, jump up and down on, and build our lives on.

- We "serve God by his Spirit." It is by the Spirit of the One who indwells us at salvation that we understand God's clear scriptural instruction. We sow to please the Spirit (Ephesians 6:8), we seek to "keep in step with the Spirit" (Galatians 5:25), we are sanctified by the Spirit (2 Thessalonians 2:13), and we have the truth revealed to us by the Spirit (1 Corinthians 2:10).
- We "boast in Christ Jesus." We understand that His death, burial, and resurrection comprise the *only* God-sent plan for our redemption. We know that no work of ours—physical, spiritual, or otherwise—can secure our adoption as sons and daughters of the Father.
- We "put no confidence in the flesh." It was the flesh that got Adam and Lot and David and Solomon and Peter and everybody else who messed up into trouble. Our confidence is not in the failing nature of depraved man but in the unfailing perfection of our Savior.

"The Spirit. Christ Jesus. And not us." If we keep that little reminder of who we should depend on in mind, we won't be threatened by Judaizers or any other "dogs" that growl at us that their way is better than God's.

Paul meant business when he wrote those harsh, clear words of warning to his brothers and sisters in Philippi. May we take them today as seriously as they were intended back then.

How Do These Verses Help Me Stand Firm?

I can use this as a reminder that there really is nothing new under the sun. For as long as there has been clear doctrine spelled out in Scripture, there have been people who feel obligated to twist it and revisit it and refashion it. I see this even today as orthodox doctrines are continually attacked in the name of inclusivism or tolerance or some other accommodating approach. I stand firm when I revisit the unchangeable truth of the gospel of Jesus Christ and reaffirm that it is only by faith in Him that I am saved.

What Has to Change?

Am I satisfied with the clear, unvarnished gospel? Or am I looking for an out—a loophole—from the absolute truth of the great message of Christ's sacrifice? If so, I'm on the way to confusion and darkness and my direction must change. I must retrace my steps to the Savior.

PHILIPPIANS 3:4–6

Though I myself have reasons for such confidence. If someone else thinks they have reasons to put confidence in the flesh, I have more: circumcised on the eighth day, of the people of Israel, of the tribe of Benjamin, a Hebrew of Hebrews; in regard to the law, a Pharisee; as for zeal, persecuting the church; as for righteousness based on the law, faultless.

What You Need To Know

"Look at me," says Paul. If anyone could have "confidence in the flesh" it was him. We've already looked at his upbringing as a strong student of Judaism under the best of rabbis. But if we look beyond that to his actions, we see someone who abhorred the followers of Christ. It was Saul (as he was then called) who gave the approval for the stoning of Stephen (Acts 8:1). Shortly thereafter, Paul became an anti-church terrorist and "began to destroy the church" (8:3). He dragged believers from their homes and had them tossed into prison. Why did Saul do this? Because his religion taught him that he was right and they were wrong. He followed the 600-plus laws of the Pharisees, and with zeal he tried to halt the Jesus people, "breathing out murderous threats against the Lord's disciples" (9:1).

We all know of people who are ardently supportive of wrong causes—and that was Saul. He believed he was right, and Christians feared him.

Testimony Time

I remember testimony time on Wednesday nights at the Christian college I attended many years ago. During that era in the 1970s we were going through the beginning stages of a turbulent time in American culture. Old taboos were being tested and new forms of questionable behavior were becoming more prevalent. Therefore, we often heard testimonies from students who had come out of such sins as drug abuse or sexual promiscuity. For some of us, who thought accidentally running a red light while driving was the height of youthful rebellion, these stories sometimes made us feel a little puny about being saved from nothing more spectacular than fighting with our siblings or listening to the Beatles with a transistor radio under the pillow so our parents didn't know.

I get a little of that "look at what I was saved from" feeling when I read Paul's recitation of his life as Saul, which caused his being a "Hebrew of the Hebrews" to degenerate into blatant persecution of our first-century brothers and sisters in Christ.

Paul was indeed a religious person in his youth. As a baby, he was circumcised, as was every son of faithful Jewish parents. He was not only of the house of Israel, but he was also of the tribe of Benjamin, making him a member of an elite Jewish family. Some contend that when he mentioned this, Paul had in mind the fact that the first king of Israel was of this tribe—and we can't miss the connection Paul's parents made when they named their little boy Saul.

Paul was one of those law-abiders called a Pharisee—they of the 600-plus laws that must be adhered to. And in his zeal he thought he was doing the right thing by persecuting this tiny sect of people who followed the man who attacked the Pharisees verbally, Jesus Christ.

So Paul's testimony time gives him a chance to let the people of Philippi know that when he spoke of the Judaizers, he knew what he was talking about. He was, indeed, their kin. He had their methodology, teaching, and tradition in his blood. He knew how the other side lived, just as my friends who experienced ungodly living in the 1970s knew how things were in the kingdom of darkness.

What about our own personal story? Are we at all like the two groups Paul introduces us to—the Judaizers or the Pharisees? We are if we think we have to add something—anything—to the pure gospel of Jesus Christ. Or if we believe that following a set of rules sets us free.

When Saul (who became Paul) met Jesus on the Damascus road and was suddenly blinded physically, the eyes of his soul were opened so he could see truth and experience freedom. No longer was he bound to the law, and no longer was he blinded by manmade restrictions.

How can we convey this message of freedom and sight to others? How can we let them know that Jesus did all the work and our task is to trust?

Perhaps the best way to let them know is by telling our story—by sharing our testimony. That is something no one can deny, and it just might be the best way to tell a world growing wary of absolutes that Jesus' story has made your story one they might want to consider for themselves.

How Do These Verses Help Me Stand Firm?

It helps me think about my own testimony—my own story—and how I can use it to share Jesus with others. In reality, my story is unassailable. No one can say, "That didn't really happen." People must deal with my words and my testimony of the change Jesus has made in my life.

What Has to Change?

Am I afraid to share my testimony? Am I afraid I will be mocked or ignored, or that I won't know how to answer tough questions? That can change with study and with prayer and with dependence on the Holy Spirit.

But whatever were gains to me I now consider loss for the sake of Christ. What is more, I consider everything a loss because of the surpassing worth of knowing Christ Jesus my Lord, for whose sake I have lost all things. I consider them garbage, that I may gain Christ and be found in him, not having a righteousness of my own that comes from the law, but that which is through faith in Christ—the righteousness that comes from God on the basis of faith.

What You Need to Know

Saul didn't know Jesus and despised those who followed His teachings. But then, in a flash (literally), he knew Jesus. Everything, including his name, changed. Paul, though blind, began praying. He got a vision from the Lord. He was filled with the Holy Spirit. He got baptized. And he began to preach. He went from searching out those who belonged to "the Way" so he could persecute them to being a part of "the Way."

Paul was transformed. He suddenly "knew Jesus." At once he realized that Jesus was "the son of God" (Acts

9:20), and he baffled his former colleagues by setting out
to prove that Jesus is the Christ. That is the "surpassing
worth of knowing Christ." It is not a stiff prayer given
like a Boy Scout oath. It is coming into a relationship
with the Son of God through faith, receiving the power
of the Spirit, and understanding the astounding change
Jesus makes. It is indeed a relationship, and Paul shows
us what it truly means to "know Jesus."

A Total Loss

Over the years we've heard the sad stories of people who,
through either mismanagement or forces out of their control, lost
everything they had worked hard to accumulate. Among these are
world-famous athletes who have earned and squandered millions.

These athletes once had it all. They were revered for their
skills and lauded by magazine writers, TV announcers, and fans
alike. And then it was gone. Some lost their money to drugs.
Some to unscrupulous investors. Some to glitzy possessions such
as jets or mansions.

The apostle Paul "lost all things" too. He admits it. But his
tradeoff was very different from the ones forced by poor decisions
on the bankrupt men and women of sports. While they are left
to squirm out of bankruptcy and somehow try to restore their
tarnished reputations, Paul revels in his loss.

And why can he feel so good about having lost everything?
Because what he lost was, in his own words, "garbage" that was
replaced by something of inestimable value.

Although Paul lost his standing as a Pharisee who prided himself on legalistic righteousness, he gained "the surpassing worth of knowing Christ Jesus my Lord." He exchanged a "righteousness of my own" for "that which is through faith in Christ."

This should lead us to do some soul-searching about what we have in this life. Are we building sandcastles in the rain by focusing our attention on actions and ideas that are less important than the "righteousness that comes from God on the basis of faith"? We are if we value personal gain and success while ignoring Jesus' call to "take up their cross and follow me" (Matthew 16:24). We are trying to profit from the worthless if we spend our time accumulating selfishly while the church and the needy are ignored. We are rushing toward spiritual bankruptcy if we seek a life of personal ease instead of one dedicated to righteousness.

The transaction Paul made that turned him from being a religious leader to being a godly servant began in a blinding flash. His transformation was immediate, and from that point on he turned his back on the "rubbish" of empty religiosity. For us, the beginning of the transaction comes when we recognize Jesus' finished work for us on the cross and trust Him as Savior. But having done that, are we willing to agree with Paul that the sake of Christ and the opportunity to "gain Christ" puts our possessions and our preferences in the "total loss" column?

This is a hard question. Paul has set the bar rather high here in this passage as he contrasts his achievements with the advantages of faith. It may take some careful reconsideration of our priorities if we indeed want to imitate the Paul we see in this passage.

Paul gave up everything he held dear to proclaim Jesus at the risk of his very life. What are we willing to declare a total loss in our lives so God's name can be glorified and His story can be told?

How Do These Verses Help Me Stand Firm?

The challenge of a Paul-like change in my life is a big thing. But I can begin by standing firm if I see little changes as my goal. Perhaps I can consider sacrificing a little time to do something good for someone else, or maybe I can increase a financial commitment to a godly cause. Small changes can eventually add up to a big change.

What Has to Change?

Is there any garbage-like thing in my life that needs to be swept away to make more room for Jesus and more time for service to Him? Is there a sacrifice I need to make for God's glory?

PHILIPPIANS 3:10–11

I want to know Christ—yes, to know the power of his resurrection and participation in his sufferings, becoming like him in his death, and so, somehow, attaining to the resurrection from the dead.

What You Need to Know

The powerful challenge Paul provides in these two verses is reflected in the deep meaning of a couple of key words: *power* and *participation*. The word *power* is used 120 times in the New Testament (Strong's Concordance). It represents a variety of meanings, including physical force, might, energy, powerful deeds, and even miraculous deeds. And then there is fellowship, which calls us to somehow take part in the sufferings of our Savior. We can in no way truly understand His suffering, for He endured a death like none other as the weight of our sin crushed Him on the cross. But Paul suggests the possibility of somehow connecting to Jesus through seeing His death as a picture of how we are to die to sin. Power and participation—two concepts that take us closer to Christ in a new way.

What Did Jesus Do?

Several years ago it was all the rage among Christians—especially young people—to wear little rubber bracelets that carried the letters WWJD, which stood for What Would Jesus Do? The idea was that as you went through a typical day, you were to try to figure out—from what you know about Him—what Jesus would do in a situation.

For instance, if you were driving along and you were late for work, think of what Jesus would do if He were driving (He probably wouldn't have left late for work). Or if you were playing basketball, think of how Jesus would guard His man. If you were at work and your boss gave you a hard time, imagine Jesus' reaction and try to emulate it. That kind of thing.

But there is a much more important consideration regarding Jesus that takes our relationship out of the realm of speculation and puts it into the arena of reality. That consideration stems from seeing what Jesus actually did when He was in His human incarnation on this planet and allowing that to guide our actions. Paul sets us an example in these two verses.

- What did Jesus do? *He was resurrected.* Paul said that he wanted to know Christ and the "power of His resurrection." All who have put their faith in Jesus "know Christ," but Paul handed down a huge challenge when he spoke of knowing the power of the resurrection. This is power of the highest order. It provides the believer with an astounding power—*dunamis* in the Greek—that suggests "power residing in a thing by virtue of its nature" (Thayer's Greek-English Lexicon). On the basis

of the fact that Jesus overcame death through resurrection, the believer becomes a new creation, gains the
peace of redemption, and receives instruction through
the Holy Spirit. Because Jesus was resurrected, the
believer is transformed by a power we can hardly begin
to imagine.

Paul wants to know this power. He wants to understand the
incredible results of this most amazing miracle. Like Paul, we will
be astounded if we spend time contemplating the "power of the
resurrection."

- What did Jesus do? *He suffered.* And Paul wants to
  cooperate with Jesus in those sufferings. To us, this is
  an almost bizarre idea. Who of us wants to take part in
  anyone's struggles? Don't we want to avoid them? We
  may not understand it, but we can see this "participation in his sufferings" by observing Paul's life. He was
  not afraid to undergo extreme persecution and even
  painful punishment for Jesus' sake. This is not an easy
  truth to contemplate.

In 2 Corinthians 1:5 Paul suggests that as Christ suffered,
we suffer. As a result, something good happens: Our comfort
overflows to others. In Romans 8:17 he reminds us that being a
co-heir with Jesus means we will "share in his sufferings."

Paul was pretty radical, don't you think? He was not in this
for the glory or the name or the fame. He was a follower of Jesus,
it seems, so he could have the joy of participating with Him in
His sufferings.

- What did Jesus do? *He died.* While our Savior died a literal death, these words of Paul here—"becoming like him in his death"—are sometimes seen as symbolic. The believer does not have to face death for sanctification to take place, but there is a sense in which we must die to sin in order to represent Christ to the world. Our willingness to die to sin is our way of conforming to death while still serving on this earth.

Now that we know what Jesus did and how Paul responded to it, perhaps we can go back to the WWJD idea. Knowing what we now know, how should we live?

First, we live with confident power as we witness for Jesus. Second, we refuse to shy away from the possibility of suffering on Jesus' behalf. And third, we agree with Paul that sin should be dead to us because we are alive with Christ.

What an agenda Paul has set forth for us as we strive to "attain to the resurrection from the dead" by resolutely seeking to live for the Savior in all we say and do.

How Do These Verses Help Me Stand Firm?

The reminder of Jesus' death for me can't help but make me stand a little firmer. First, because I stand amazed that Jesus did that for me. And second, because I see the depth of His sacrifice, I am spurred to respond in action and love for His sake.

What Has to Change?

What is my view of the Christian life? Do I see it as a place of ease? Of being comfortable? Or do I need to see it as a place of cross-bearing when necessary?

PHILIPPIANS 3:12

Not that I have already obtained all this, or have already arrived at my goal, but I press on to take hold of that for which Christ Jesus took hold of me.

What You Need to Know

Nobody's perfect. Let's get that idea out in the open right away. The Bible lets us know that while we are sanctified in our position before God—that is, our salvation allows God to see us as having never sinned because of Jesus—our real-life experience is marred by our imperfection. "My sin is always before me," David said (Psalm 51:3). Paul, our companion in this study, said, "I am unspiritual, sold as a slave to sin. . . . For what I want to do I do not do, but what I hate I do" (Romans 7:14–15). James put it like this: "We all stumble in many ways" (James 3:2). Yet while perfection is unattainable, we keep moving toward a vigorous attempt at a righteousness that pleases our Savior and shines glory on Him for others to see.

Under Construction

While I was writing this book, one of my first college professors, Dr. James Grier, died at the age of eighty. Dr. Grier was a brilliant Bible teacher and scholar. When I had him as a philosophy professor in my freshman year, I was overwhelmed with his erudition (even though I don't think I knew what that word meant at the time).

Over the years, every time I would hear Dr. Grier expound on Scripture and speak of his love for Jesus, I was in awe. He had a depth of knowledge and experience that challenged all of us who were in his presence.

That's why I was not surprised to learn that even in his final time on earth he continued to seek to know the Lord more and more. Doug Phillips, one of Dr. Grier's longtime friends, wrote this about his final days: "With even greater focus and purpose, he turned to the Scriptures, and through them to the Lord Jesus himself." It seems that this great man of God, who could hold us spellbound with his exposition, felt as if he had not "already obtained" the high marks Paul discusses in Philippians 3:7–11. He realized that he had not "arrived at [his] goal." Dr. Grier often referred to himself as the Old Pilgrim, but he knew that only when he arrived at the Celestial City would he be made complete.

It is amazing how many great men and women of God understand the concept Paul is describing here. As believers in Jesus and as pilgrims on the road to heaven, we have a responsibility to learn, to grow, to seek God. But we will not reach our full level of sanctification on this side of the great reward of heaven. We are all under construction.

At one time Paul thought he had arrived—back in his days of being a well-educated Pharisee. But then the flash of light and everything changed. He was introduced to a new learning curve that was not dedicated to the law of Moses but to the prospect of "knowing Christ." And although Paul received a starter course on the backside of the desert and a crash course about the Savior on his various missionary journeys, he realized that until he arrived in glory, he would never know Jesus as he could. No wonder he often spoke of being with Christ as "far better." Then and only then would he have the perfect knowledge of our perfect Savior.

Paul was under construction, as we are, in a project that cannot be completed in this life. Yet just as Dr. Grier kept growing and learning right up until his death, so are we to "press on to take hold of that for which Christ Jesus took hold of [us]."

Press on. That is our marching order.

Press on to know Jesus better and better each day.

Press on to find new reasons to stand in awe of God's majesty.

Press on to understand how to work in unison and harmony with our fellow believers in the great tasks God has called us to do.

Press on to find ways to love our neighbors as ourselves.

Press on to love the Lord our God with all our hearts, souls, and minds.

Paul left the end of his "press on" message rather open-ended. He said, "I press on to take hold of that for which Christ Jesus took hold of me." What are you pressing on to take hold of?

How Does This Verse Help Me Stand Firm?

It easier to give up than to press on. I need Paul's encouragement to continue to seek the righteousness of God. I need the reminder that this man of many struggles was not about to cave in to the pressure to ride the easy road to heaven.

What Has to Change?

When was the last time I pressed on? When was the last time I decided to chuck the hard work and drift? Following Christ is not for drifters. It's for people with the courage to keep up the chase toward worthy goals. Is that me?

PHILIPPIANS 3:13–14

*Brothers and sisters, I do not consider myself yet
to have taken hold of it. But one thing I do: Forgetting
what is behind and straining toward what is ahead,
I press on toward the goal to win the prize for which
God has called me heavenward in Christ Jesus.*

What You Need to Know

We don't have any record that Paul was an athlete, but we do know that he loved using sports analogies to make his points.

In 1 Corinthians 9:24–27 he said we have to "run [the race] to get the prize" and "I do not fight like a boxer beating the air."

In 2 Timothy 4:6–8 he spoke of the importance of having "finished the race."

In 2 Timothy 2:5 he said, "Anyone who competes as an athlete does not receive the victor's crown except by competing according to the rules."

In 1 Timothy 4:7–8 he told his readers to "train yourself to be godly."

And now, in Philippians 3:13–14, he sounds like a coach giving instructions to his track athlete. A runner focuses on one thing alone: the finish line. He doesn't turn around and look at where he's been. He leans into the race, "straining" toward the goal. Paul knew the rules of sprinting, and he turned them into a great illustration of what it means to press on.

Don't Look Back

Satchel Paige, famous baseball pitcher from the latter days of the Negro Leagues and the early integrated days of the major leagues, said it best, "Don't look back. Something might be gaining on you."

For Paul, the idea was not just that we shouldn't look back ("forgetting what is behind") but that we should not look anywhere but ahead as we move forward for God.

There is comfort in this passage, because Paul reminds us that he is not some pedestal-climbing saint talking down to the puny pew-sitters. He calls us "brothers and sisters." Just as he did at the beginning of the book (1:12), he sees us as siblings in the family, all running the same race to glory.

So, what is Brother Paul telling his Philippian siblings—and us? He is telling us that we are in an extremely important race, and he knows how we should run that race.

Paul, our brother, is our track coach here, and he has one bit of advice for us. After he reminds us of what he told us in verse 12—that he has not yet arrived in his walk with the Lord—he puts on his track coach hat and says, "Okay, team. Here's what I do."

Sometimes we get far too much advice when we are about to do something. Perhaps we have a mentor, and he or she overloads us with dos and don'ts that only confuse us when it comes time for the action to begin. But Paul, like a wise veteran coach, whittles down his advice to just one thing: Don't look back. "Forgetting what is behind and straining toward what is ahead," he says.

Can you see yourself in this race? You are focused on only one thing: The finish line and the tape that is stretched across the line. You are not worried about what is chasing you—those troubles that want to run you down. You are not concerned with those around you—whether they are yelling encouragement or disparagement. You are looking straight ahead. You are straining forward. You are pushing yourself to reach that goal—and nothing is going to slow you down.

When we run a race, we know ahead of time why we are putting on the shoes and putting forth the effort. Perhaps it's a local 5k race and we are challenging ourselves to get into shape for the physical advantage. When we were younger, perhaps we ran races with our buddies to prove that we were faster. In Paul's analogy of racing, he is probably referring to the Isthmian Games, which were somewhat like our Olympics. The race was run to win a prize, most likely a wreath.

But we are running for the "prize for which God has called [us] heavenward." We are straining ahead as a way of staying on course for our final destination. It is having a single-minded purpose of pleasing the Lord as we head for our heavenly home.

As Christians, our destination is secure. We don't have to compete for that. Christ's death and resurrection have secured that for those who believe. But as we make our way, our goal is Jesus—to know Him, as Paul earlier mentioned, and to serve Him. It is our calling as believers, and if we "look back" or get sidetracked, we lose the opportunity to maximize our relationship with Him.

As we run the race, we need to think about commitment and diligence in our Christ-service. Do we get sidetracked by relationships? Do the burdens of life itself weigh us down and make us less likely to run well?

If you have ever run a race, you know how this works. Perhaps even your body itself becomes a distraction as this or that muscle hurts and your mind says, "You need to stop because this is not fun anymore." Or maybe you see an opponent gaining on you or passing you, and you feel like giving up. It could be that you recall, "Well, last time I ran, I didn't do so well," and you start talking yourself into stepping off the course and grabbing a comfy seat.

It is at those times in our lifelong spiritual race that we have to keep Coach Paul's words coursing through our minds and hearts: "I had not arrived either—but one thing to keep in mind: Forget the past, don't get distracted, and press on for the Lord's glory because that is your calling from God."

How Do These Verses Help Me Stand Firm?

My past can bring me down if I let it. Standing firm happens when I recognize my past situation but then put it in God's hands and not try to carry it myself. Pressing on and not looking back is part of that—as is casting my burdens on Jesus, who asked me to do that.

What Has to Change?

What am I carrying around with me from the past that is a weight? What is the best way to drop that weight and free myself to run the race more easily?

PHILIPPIANS 3:15–16

*All of us, then, who are mature should take such a view
of things. And if on some point you think differently,
that too God will make clear to you. Only let us
live up to what we have already attained.*

What You Need to Know

When the apostle Paul says, "All of us, then, who are mature should take such a view of things," he is emphasizing the dependability of Scripture. If we are mature believers, we will trust the words of God's inspired book. Paul also assures us that the Holy Spirit is available to help us understand the Word if we listen to His promptings and allow Him to enlighten our study of the Bible.

A Little Maturity Here

In the first few years after I was out of college, I was a high school basketball coach at a Christian school. It was a remarkable experience as I got to know a bunch of really great young men, many of whom continue to be spiritual leaders in their homes and families today. And we won quite a few basketball games in the process.

When I coached, I expected my guys to be paragons of virtue at school, and I expected them to be good examples to the other students. I wanted them to "live up to" a high standard.

One day, though, some of my paragons of virtue reverted to mischievous-teenage-boy status and did something that caused embarrassment to the team as a whole and me as the coach. Nothing illegal or anything, but when I walked into school on the Monday morning after the incident and was met by the principal, who said, "Did you hear what *your boys* did on Friday night?" I knew I had to do something. See, I was expecting "mature" actions from these guys, but they tended to "think differently" than I did about the issue of um, "decorating" fellow students' cars in the parking lot at our homecoming banquet. So I had to "make clear" to them my disappointment by allowing them to sit on the bench next to me for one game.

Paul wanted to see maturity in the lives of his Christian brothers and sisters in Philippi, but he knew that not everyone would agree on what that standard of maturity was. When Paul wrote about being "mature," he was speaking to church members who needed to understand what "being made perfect" (3:12 NIV, 1984) meant.

There is some disagreement on whether or not Paul was addressing an actual problem in the church on this issue—some scholars say a group of people were suggesting that Christians could reach actual perfection this side of heaven. Regardless of that, though, we do know that Paul was telling his friends in Philippi that maturity means desiring the prize of knowing God and seeking to serve Him. Growing in maturity leads to greater servanthood as we are guided by God's love and His instructions through the power of the Holy Spirit.

We are all at different levels of maturity. Yet none of us is expected to remain stagnant or to stop growing. Whatever level of maturity we have "already attained," as Paul puts it, we should continue to move ahead—or move forward, as he earlier said in his race analogy. When we do, we step into the next level of maturity.

With that pattern established, we will always be making progress, and we will be living up to our calling in Christ.

How Do These Verses Help Me Stand Firm?

It challenges me to move toward spiritual maturity, which includes a right view of Scripture and a willingness to trust the inner promptings of the indwelling Holy Spirit. And who stands firmer in the face of life's circumstances than the mature?

What Has to Change?

Am I willing to accept the clear teachings of Scripture about such things as the concept of perfection and the race to seek God's best? Am I willing to trust the Spirit of God to guide me into truth and into right life action?

PHILIPPIANS 3:17

Join together in following my example, brothers and sisters, and just as you have us as a model, keep your eyes on those who live as we do.

What You Need to Know

Paul, as a young man (then called Saul), was a student of the rabbi Gamaliel. Because of this, he understood the Jewish teaching tradition. As a student matured under the tutelage of a rabbi, he became a disciple (a talmid) of that leader. The goal of the disciple was not simply to learn information from the rabbi, though he gained much of that through his study of the Torah. His main goal was to become like his teacher. This meant that imitation was a major component of the learning process. The disciple of the rabbi observed his teacher—and not just in the classroom. He watched and listened to all the rabbi did and said so he could become like him. Eventually that led the student to be so imitative of the rabbi that he himself became a teacher and passed on his knowledge to others. It is easy to see how this upbringing in Paul's life could be reflected in what he is saying in Philippians 3:17.

Teacher to Student: Follow Me

There are many schoolteachers in my family. My mother, in fact, was my fourth grade teacher in a public school. My brother taught at my high school and was an Ohio Baseball Hall of Fame coach. I taught for eight years before becoming an editor and writer. Two of my daughters are schoolteachers. My son-in-law taught for several years, and a nephew is following my footsteps as an English teacher.

One thing I am proudest about in our family's record as teachers is that (as far as I have seen or heard) we all have been known for being good examples to our students. We have sought not to simply convey information but also to show our students how to live—how to handle adversity, how to be kind yet firm, how to treat everyone the same.

That's what good teachers do. They don't just spout facts and grade papers. They expect to leave an imprint on their students. They want to leave a legacy of learning that can be followed and imitated.

That's similar to the tradition the apostle Paul grew up in as he learned and grew in his religious life under the teaching of his Jewish instructors. As a maturing Jewish disciple, he would have realized that to get the most out of his education, he must watch his rabbi closely and learn to imitate him.

Thus, Paul used the illustration of example and imitation from his own days as a student to explain that the people in Philippi could learn a lot about how they were to live by watching and imitating him. Just as Paul probably did with Gamaliel, his teacher, he wanted the people in the church to listen to him, to watch what he did, to observe how he reacted so they would know how they should live.

What a challenge Paul's words are to all of us in the church. As a rabbi lived by the Torah and the other laws of the Jewish system, we live by the revealed totality of God's Word. We seek to live by its precepts and principles and teachings in order to be a worthy example to others who are watching and learning from us.

As a high school teacher, I knew that my students were watching me. As a coach, I knew that the words I used in the locker room and at practice, and the attitudes I showed toward the referees and the opponents, would be mirrored by my athletes. I knew that even as I taught English in the classroom, my attitude toward learning and studying and accuracy would rub off on them.

By God's grace, many of my students imitated what they were taught by me, by my fellow teachers, and by their parents and grew into productive, godly adults.

And by God's grace, perhaps we can be like Paul in setting examples for those who follow in our pathway—setting admirable examples in life, in love, and in learning. As we do, we can see our circle of Christian brothers and sisters mature, enabling the fellowship of believers to expand for the honor and glory of God.

How Does This Verse Help Me Stand Firm?

The more I follow Paul's lead, the more likely I am to live in a godly way. That will not only help me stand firm but it will also influence others, through God's leading, to do the same.

What Has to Change?

Have I learned enough of Paul's life and words to imitate his example? Am I willing and eager to have people follow my lead? Or do I feel I'm falling a bit short of being that kind of person?

PHILIPPIANS 3:18-19

For, as I have often told you before and now tell you again even with tears, many live as enemies of the cross of Christ. Their destiny is destruction, their god is their stomach, and their glory is in their shame. The mind is set on earthly things.

What You Need to Know

When Jesus changed Saul into Paul on the Damascus road, He changed not just his thinking about matters of religion: He changed his heart. Jesus changed him from a man who persecuted others for their faith in Christ to a man whose entire life was devoted to godly teaching and rescuing people from certain eternal despair without Jesus. The words of these verses came from the inspiration of the Holy Spirit, but they also came from the heart of a man who cared deeply for the lost.

Moist Eyes

Something on Paul's mind is breaking his heart when he looks over the landscape of the first-century church—and tears fill his eyes as he writes about it. This was apparently an ongoing concern for Paul, for he not only discussed it with the church when he visited them at Philippi, but he also feels compelled to bring it up again in his letter to them.

Parents of children who have walked away from truth and integrity and godliness truly understand this kind of thinking. They recall those times when they tried to explain a truth to their children—hoping to spare them from the trouble that wrong living will bring. And those parents realize—with tears—that the issues they spoke with their children about in the past are still affecting them, still destroying them and leading them away from successful living.

There seems to be a parallel in this passage as Paul addresses the church. His concern is about many who, as he says, "live as enemies of the cross of Christ" (v. 18). He says it brings tears to his eyes as he writes these words. But what enemies is he talking about? He could be speaking of the same people he referred to earlier as "those dogs" (v. 2), or he could be referring to the Judaizers, who wanted to add to the gospel, ripping any effectiveness from Christ's death, burial, and resurrection.

The truth is, we don't know exactly what group caused so much sadness for Paul. But we do know that the characteristics he described still exist in people today—and can be a danger to us.

Think of what Paul is doing in this marvelous passage: He is warning us not to be sidetracked by the pleasures or promises offered by the enemies of the cross. Do not be misled by those who can't stand Jesus' sacrifice, he is saying. Don't be tempted by evil and its fool's gold of false gifts to reject the most glorious existence ever. Those who do not understand the gospel or who have heard the story but are not willing to accept Jesus' forgiveness are settling for citizenship in a foreign land that offers only temporary pleasures while they are being offered a land of endless joy and bliss.

Can there be a more up-to-date picture of what those outside of faith in Christ celebrate today? When Paul mentions that "their god is their belly," does that not sound like those who want to characterize Christianity as narrow and joyless while fulfilling their every lust and appetite with hopeless immorality?

When he talks of those "whose glory is their shame," can you not see the almost daily reports of those who flaunt the purity called for in Scripture by bragging about shameless lives of sexual sins or wild parties or increasingly filthy language?

When Paul writes about folks whose minds are "on earthly things," it's not hard to think of those who completely reject any influence of God in their lives—opting instead for atheism or agnosticism or worldview concepts that leave no room for the divine.

The contrast between godliness and ungodliness in this heartfelt passage of Scripture could not be clearer. Paul pours out his soul as he sorrows for those who reject God and His wonderful plan for the world and for eternity.

Think about Paul's passion. Think of how much he cares for those on the outside of faith looking in. Do we share his concern?

Are there tears in our eyes for those who not only "live as enemies of the cross of Christ," but who also discover that their "destiny is destruction"?

How Do These Verses Help Me Stand Firm?

I have it—this grand and glorious gift Paul wishes all to receive. I have been redeemed and washed by Jesus' blood. Then why do I—why do so many of us—stand wobbly-kneed before the naysayers and new atheists and others who pooh-pooh my faith? This passage can encourage me to renew my faith, to recommit my heart to what I know is truth. And truth can set me so free of the enemies of the cross that I can strengthen my stand for the gospel.

What Has to Change?

When was the last time I prayed for the lost? When was the last time I shed a tear for someone who seems to be on a one-way road to hell's destruction? Can I learn from Paul to care more deeply for souls headed for darkness?

PHILIPPIANS 3:20-21

But our citizenship is in heaven. And we eagerly await a Savior from there, the Lord Jesus Christ, who, by the power that enables him to bring everything under his control, will transform our lowly bodies so that they will be like his glorious body.

What You Need to Know

Heaven. We long to know more about it than we do. We long to know exactly what it looks like. And perhaps most of all we wish we knew what our loved ones who have trusted Christ and have been called home by the Lord are actually doing there. But God has left those facts behind the curtain. What He has revealed to us, though, should encourage us. We know that our Savior is there—the One we all long to see face to face. And we know that somehow, in a way more miraculous than our earth-based brains can imagine, we will be transformed. What we cherish here on this side—our "lowly bodies"—will be changed into something "glorious." That's enough to whet our appetites for heaven, isn't it?

The Choice of Two Citizenships

I love to travel and visit exotic or interesting places. I have been privileged to visit several countries, mostly on some kind of ministry or missions trip, and I have found many that I absolutely love.

Jamaica is a clear favorite. Being from, let's just say, a less-than-tropical state like Michigan, it is indeed a treat to get off the plane in Jamaica and realize that no matter what time of year it is, the weather will be "No problem, mon!" And besides that, the Jamaicans are magnificent people.

I loved visiting Israel and seeing the land of the Bible.

The Philippines is a special place with special people and a fascinating culture. My wife and I lived there for a school year and grew very fond of that vibrant country.

In the UK, I couldn't get enough of the rolling hills and calm pastures with flocks of grazing sheep.

Spain has enough beauty in its architecture alone to keep a traveler intrigued for a long time.

But no matter how many times I travel to other countries, and no matter how much I enjoy my visits, there is nothing like getting off that final flight back in Grand Rapids and realizing that I am *home*—back in the city where I reside and safely back in the country of my citizenship.

We don't spend much time thinking about things this way in regard to our eternal destiny, but whether we live in Montego Bay or Jerusalem or Manila or London or Madrid or Grand Rapids, these places are not really our home. These places are not where our permanent citizenship is found.

Our citizenship, Paul reminds us, is in heaven.

Heaven is where we will spend the endless, perfect, awesome, matchless, and splendiferous eternity that Jesus earned for us through His sacrifice on the cross and His resurrection from the dead. This is our true home, our genuine residence, our real, final destination.

Contrast this with the sad news Paul gives in this passage about those who oppose the cross and whose minds and hearts are so married to the earth that they forfeit the possibility of eternal bliss in heaven. Paul spells out the two possibilities available to all: earthly things versus a citizenship in heaven.

The tears that accompany Paul's explanation about those enemies of the cross present a striking irony when we consider that heaven is a place where there will be no tears (Revelation 7:17). Our only time to feel compassion for the lost and to share with them the truth about their future destruction if they don't turn to Christ is here in this land of tears.

As Paul reminds us in this passage, heaven will be a place full of glory and filled with the presence of our Savior, the Lord Jesus Christ. It is the place where our all-powerful God will "transform our lowly bodies" into bodies that will be like the glorious body of our risen Savior.

So where are you in this picture of lands of contrast? Where is your citizenship? Where is the citizenship of those you love? Can you say, can they say, without tears and with matchless expectation: Our citizenship is in heaven?

No matter how many places you visit on earth, your ultimate destination is the one that is truly important.

How Do These Verses Help Me Stand Firm?

How firm is my assurance that I have trusted Christ's work on my behalf, enabling my entrance into God's grand eternal home?

What Has to Change?

Am I sure of heaven? Are there people close to me who need to be asked that question? Am I more interested in comfort in this life than I am in the ultimate perfection of the next?

PHILIPPIANS 4

SOME TEACHING, SOME THANKING, AND A KIND GOOD-BYE

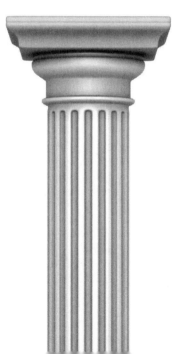

PHILIPPIANS 4:1

*Therefore, my brothers and sisters, you whom
I love and long for, my joy and crown, stand
firm in the Lord in this way, dear friends!*

What You Need to Know

What a fascinating study it is to see how the Bible
uses this term "stand firm," which Paul incorporates
twice as he attempts to build up the church he loves so
much! There are at least thirty-five places in the NIV
translation where these two words are used together. Let's
look at some of the ways the Holy Spirit uses the term to
encourage God's people:

- Moses to the people of Israel: "Do not be afraid.
  Stand firm" (Exodus 14:13). This was his com-
  mand as the Egyptian army was bearing down
  on them. His promise? "The Egyptians you see
  today you will never see again." Wow!
- The Spirit of the LORD to Israel's army standing before a vast army of enemies: "Stand firm

---

and see the deliverance the LORD will give you" (2 Chronicles 20:17). The Israelites didn't even have to fight. They sang their way to victory!

- David to the people: "The plans of the LORD stand firm forever" (Psalm 33:11).
- Ethan to the people: "[The LORD's] love stands firm forever" (Psalm 89:2).
- The psalmist to the people: "Your word, LORD, is eternal; it stands firm in the heavens" (Psalm 119:89).
- Paul to the Corinthians: "Stand firm. Let nothing move you" (1 Corinthians 15:58). For God, His promises and His Word are firm and immoveable. We, however, must do this—that is, stand firm—by His power.

When They Don't Stand Firm

What warmth and love are spelled out in the first verse of Philippians 4:

"My brothers and sisters."

"Whom I love."

"Whom I long for."

"My joy and crown."

"Dear friends."

These terms of endearment cannot help but give us a glimpse into how much Paul cared for his friends in Philippi. It is this love that has him pleading for them to stand firm.

But let's think for a moment about how this kind of concern can also cause us great pain and sorrow if those we love and care for do not stand firm.

I think about this in regard to parents who love their children and have poured their love and spiritual direction into them, yet must watch almost helplessly as those youngsters refuse to stand firm. The wobbly ground of postmodern thinking has convinced them that trusting the ancient words of the Bible is too confining, and they have succumbed to the kinds of thinking that Paul addressed at the end of chapter 3.

A stand-firm believer recognizes and reveres God's plan for the family as spelled out long ago in Genesis 2—a man united to his wife in a marriage where children are "a heritage from the Lord" who are cared for with unquestioned love. Those who do not stand firm bend to the world's ways of cohabitation and a lackadaisical view of their responsibility to their offspring.

A stand-firm believer values meeting together with fellow believers in church and recognizes the value of listening to the Word preached, to singing hymns and songs together, and to finding valuable work in the body of Christ. One who does not stand firm thinks it is old-fashioned to be tied down to a church and all its traditions.

A stand-firm believer avoids corrupt communication, gets along with others as much as is possible, and shows compassionate care and love for his or her neighbors. Those who do not stand firm will not care how they speak, will look out for themselves over others, and will not be concerned with their neighbors, no matter who they are.

A stand-firm believer understands the importance of prayer in his or her life, recognizes the value of Bible reading and time with God, and seeks to enhance his or her relationship with Him independently of others. One who does not stand firm sees little value in talking to God, views the Bible as irrelevant in all but the most essential matters, and pays only passing attention to our heavenly Father.

Twice Paul pleads with his friends in Philippi to "stand firm." The first time, he asks them to "stand firm in the one Spirit" contending for the faith (1:27). Here in chapter 4, he seems to be suggesting that they "stand firm in the Lord" in regard to their lifestyle.

The concept of standing firm is a popular one in Scripture. As mentioned earlier, the New International Version uses the term thirty-five times. What a challenge that can be for us as we recognize the importance of not following a world system that seems intent on knocking the props out from under us. As we look around at a society that wants us to abandon our morals, our foundation, and our faith in favor of a philosophy that says there is no truth and even that there is no need for God, we must stand firm.

This is not easy. Over the centuries, people have been abused, persecuted, and even put to death for standing firm for the gospel. In our own day, in certain places, we have seen Christians taken from their homes and imprisoned for sticking with their convictions. In our own part of the world, we have seen growing opposition to those who stand for good and for God. Schoolchildren have been punished for doing reports on Bible topics. College students have been ostracized by their professors for being willing to argue the cause of Christ. Companies have suffered financial loss when they ran up against government rules that violated the owner's biblical beliefs. Athletes have been ridiculed and berated for their outspoken faith in Jesus Christ. Politicians have been told to keep their beliefs private.

And you and I—what about us? How have we had to stand firm, refusing to cave in to ungodly thinking?

"Dear friends, stand firm." This was Paul's plea for his friends, and it is still our Savior's request for us. Stand firm for Jesus and watch Him provide us the strength and courage we need.

How Does This Verse Help Me Stand Firm?

This reminder should be my motto in a wishy-washy world. Stand firm. Stand strong. Stand! Should I fail to stand firm on the foundation of God's gospel, His Word, and the power of His Spirit, I run the risk of being washed away in the tsunami of change that is sweeping our culture.

What Has to Change?

Am I committed to truth? Am I committed to righteousness? Am I committed to a strong, vibrant relationship with God? Do I really want to stand firm today to ensure a life that sets an example of godliness and celebrates my citizenship in heaven?

PHILIPPIANS 4:2–3

I plead with Euodia and I plead with Syntyche to be of the same mind in the Lord. Yes, and I ask you, my true companion, help these women since they have contended at my side in the cause of the gospel, along with Clement and the rest of my co-workers, whose names are in the book of life.

What You Need to Know

Nobody likes to be called on the carpet—especially in a public forum. So it could be problematic for Paul to make such an open declaration of the situation between these two women in the church at Philippi. Often church leaders make a problem worse when they handle it incorrectly. Paul, however, takes some steps that are careful and helpful. We don't get to hear a final report on the matter, but we can look to Paul's words as a guide for similar tough situations. Let's look at what he did:

- Paul kept his remarks about both women equal: "I plead with Euodia and I plead with Syntyche." Small matter, perhaps, but he showed care in how he addressed them.

- He didn't cast aspersions at them or even reveal the cause of the problem. He kept attention on himself by his "I plead" statement. And he didn't harshly tell them to stop whatever it was they were doing. Instead he softly suggested a solution: "Be of the same mind in the Lord."
- He complimented the women. He did this by reminding the church of past times when the two women had worked beside him in the gospel effort. This warm reminder surely caused smiles of remembrance even during a bit of a correction.
- He enlisted the help of a respected person. The "true companion" was, it seems, a man of esteem among the people. Paul knew him well enough to know he would handle things properly.

It's not easy to restore those in error, but it helps if it is done in a godly way, as Paul demonstrates.

Leave Your Agendas at the Door

When we walk into the sanctuary at church on Sunday, what do we bring with us besides our Bibles? Do we haul our agendas along with us?

Perhaps we have an issue that we think is very important to the success of our church and it has been stewing in our minds for a long time. Let's say, just as an example, that our agenda item is this: The song service is too long, and the worship leader makes us stand up too much. So we haul that agenda with us and plop it down beside us as the service moves along. We have even brought a stopwatch with us this week, just to make sure we have the evidence we need. And sure enough, this week's singing is even longer than last week's—and the folks up front make the congregation stand up the whole time.

Something has to be done.

So we grab our agenda and make a beeline for a friend after church to share it with her (we "share" things at this church). But when we lay it all out for our friend—let's call her Mandy—she does not agree. In fact, she would like to see us sing a couple more songs each Sunday.

Suddenly, we have dueling agendas. Ours and Mandy's. And by the time next week rolls around, we've each enlisted several people who agree with us, and we've started to split up the church into two sides on this issue.

Silly? Of course. Unrealistic? Absolutely not. God's work has been shut down completely among a body of believers by sillier agendas than this.

We don't know what agendas Euodia and Syntyche hauled around with them at First Church of Philippi, but we can be pretty certain they stood on opposite sides of some issue. Can you imagine Paul's reaction when Epaphroditus sat down with him in Rome and said, "Uh, Paul, we've got a little problem with a couple of the women. You remember Euodia and Syntyche, don't you? Well, they are mad at each other about the color of the new curtains for the windows." (Okay, we don't know what the issue was, but we can be certain it was not doctrinal or Paul wouldn't have asked them to agree about it.)

So in his letter, Paul pleaded with these two women to set aside their agendas and "be of the same mind in the Lord." And he went beyond that. He asked one of the men in the church, one he called a "true companion," to come alongside these sisters in the Lord and help them. Paul knew Euodia and Syntyche to be valuable helpers in the cause of Christ, and he wanted to restore them to that position.

What would happen in your church if everyone were to "be of the same mind in the Lord"? This might at times seem an impossibility, but it is a constant theme of Paul's. In chapter one he said he expected them to "stand firm in the one Spirit, striving together as one for the faith of the gospel" (v. 27). That is what we should strive for in our church, and that is why we must leave our agendas at home.

Think for a moment about what it means for a body of believers to center their lives and their shared efforts around one single goal: To glorify and worship God as they proclaim the gospel. Imagine what it would be like to go into church each week with everyone focused on that clearly defined goal and willing to overlook minor differences to achieve it.

And think about this: Might you be Euodia? Could you be Syntyche? (And, guys, this includes you.) Could your pastor or your fellow church members be pleading with God right now for you and those with whom you are at odds to "be of the same mind in the Lord"? If so, put down that agenda and pick up the plan God has carefully spelled out for all of us: Love the Lord with all your heart, soul, and mind. And love your neighbor as yourself.

Now there's an agenda we can all agree on!

How Do These Verses Help Me Stand Firm?

Can this serve as a reminder for me not to show up at church next time looking for nits to pick? Imagine how firm our worshiping body of believers would be if trust of one another and belief in God's ability to guide the church were hallmarks of our church. I want to remember chapter 3, verse 15: "If on some point you think differently, that too God will make clear to you."

What Has to Change?

What is my favorite agenda item that gets me steamed up at church? Is my item more important than the unity of the believers (2:2)? What can I do to help others I worship with see the big picture and not the tiny personal agendas?

PHILIPPIANS 4:4

Rejoice in the Lord always. I will say it again: Rejoice!

What You Need to Know

The word joy is found five times in Philippians:

"In all my prayers for all of you, I always pray with joy" (1:4). Ever think about doing that: Praying with joy?

"Convinced of this, I know that I will remain, and I will continue with all of you for your progress and joy in the faith" (1:25). Ever considered the progress of your faith as a matter of joy?

"Make my joy complete by being like-minded" (2:2). Ever contemplated how much joy is brought to the church and its leaders by unity?

"Welcome him in the Lord with great joy" (2:29). Ever celebrate a returning missionary with great joy?

"My brothers and sisters . . . my joy and crown" (4:1) Ever thought of your fellow church-goers as your joy?

And then there is rejoice, a close relative of joy.

"I rejoice" (1:18). Paul rejoiced because the gospel was preached.

"I am glad and rejoice" (2:17). Paul rejoiced in being a sacrifice.

"You too should be glad and rejoice with me" (2:18). Paul didn't want to rejoice alone.

"Rejoice in the Lord!" (3:1). Paul knew what to rejoice about.

"Rejoice in the Lord always" (4:4). Paul knew he could never run out of things to rejoice about.

"I rejoiced greatly . . . that at last you renewed your concern" (4:10). Paul could even rejoice in the care he received from others.

Let's Try This!

Sometimes when I read Paul's story, I think, *What is it with this guy?* With all the stuff he went through, how can he always be so happy? How can he be sitting there in Rome—after a trip that nearly cost him his life, and after being under house arrest while writing to a group of people he wishes he was with—and still fill his writing with such upbeat messages?

Paul is all "grace and peace" and "thank you" and "affection" and "what does it matter" as he charges his way through his inspired letter to the folks back home. He seems to be the master of the silver lining. It's almost as if we should call him "the happy apostle."

And here it is again in Philippians 4. He has just had to reprimand a couple of old friends and ask another friend to assist in restoring them in order to rescue the church from further damage—and then he jumps right back into the joy boat.

While many of us at that point would be ready to say, "Man, this is hard. I wish I didn't have to keep telling these people how to act," Paul immediately says, "Rejoice in the Lord always." And as if we might not have caught it the first time: "I will say it again: Rejoice!"

Rejoice not just once. Rejoice times two.

Let's try to think about this in regard to the days of our lives.

You wake up in the morning facing another day of getting up early, going to that same job again, dealing with those same situations again, and hoping that your salary is enough to cover all of those bills again.

At that point, do you think: "Rejoice in the Lord always. I will say it again: Rejoice!"?

You come home from another day of work, and you are met at the door with a houseful of issues to contend with. The plumbing is refusing to work as designed. The kids all have to be in different places at the same time. Your spouse needs a little of your time, and you have too little to give. The bills seem to grow larger as they sit on the desk. And you just wish you had fifteen minutes in front of *SportsCenter* with the dog resting calmly on your lap.

Somehow Paul's words echo through your mind, and you wonder how he does it.

Perhaps J. B. Phillips can help. He penned what is called *The New Testament in Modern English*, and while the copyright date of 1958 isn't exactly modern anymore, Phillips' translation of Philippians 4:4 is timely and helpful: "Delight yourselves in God, yes, find your joy in him at all times."

While we normally look around us for something that will bring us joy—whether it is a good job or a happy family or money in the bank or a nice garden or our team winning lots of games—Phillips helps us direct our thinking to something so much greater: "Delight yourselves in God."

The great thing about this is that it allows us to think as Paul thought all those years ago. To delight in the Lord as the basis of our search for contentment and happiness means that we concentrate on the following—some of which come right out of this letter to the Philippians:

- Delight in the fact that Jesus left heaven's glories to come here and be your Savior.
- Delight in the promise that the Lord has prepared a grand home for us in heaven.
- Delight in the reality that our salvation in Jesus promises us an abundant life.
- Delight in Jesus' compassion for us—shown on the cross and shown in His love as a sandaled earth visitor.
- Delight in the Lord, who is the creator of heaven and earth yet who knows you by name and watches over you with endless love.
- Delight in Jesus, who is God with us—our Savior and our example.

See, Paul is telling us to think about the many, many ways that delighting in Jesus is far better than, as he will tell us in the very next verse, worrying. And he even goes further with it. Delight in the Lord and "find your joy in him," as J. B. Phillips says.

When we look for joy in our Savior and not in our changing, fragile circumstances, we have an unchanging, powerful Source.

The joy found in our Savior is not predicated on the Dow Jones average, the price of crude oil, the grades our kids get in school, the figures on our paycheck stub, the size of our house, or the professionalism of our boss.

Paul could "Rejoice in the Lord always" because he was looking past those negative circumstances that could have frightened him and kept him bitter. He looked past them because he was pursuing Jesus. He was delighting in the One who changed his life in a blinding flash on a road in Syria.

When was the last time someone took a good look at you and said, "Wow! That is one satisfied person!" If it has been too long since you looked the part of a born-again child of God, then it's time to jump into Paul's joy boat.

"Rejoice in the Lord always. I will say it again: Rejoice!"

How Does This Verse Help Me Stand Firm?

It's easy to see how rejoicing in the Lord and standing firm go together. If I can't stand firm for God after praising Him, I've got no spiritual legs.

What Has to Change?

How much do I like to rejoice? Whether I have a good singing voice or not, how often does praise music escape my lips? When was the last time I bowed my head in gratitude to send thankful words toward heaven?

PHILIPPIANS 4:5

Let your gentleness be evident to all. The Lord is near.

What You Need to Know

What kind of a person do you think Paul was? We know how tough-minded he was before he trusted Jesus—he was nothing if not nasty and dangerous to those who disagreed with him. But the redeemed Paul—what was he like? From all that we read in the New Testament, we know that he had to be someone who took challenges head-on and was not afraid of the consequences of actions others might disagree with. Yet in this letter he calls for those who follow Christ to have their "gentleness be evident to all." Combining both of those, it seems that Paul must have taken a "tough and tender" approach. His life seemed to say, Sure there are times to be strong, but those with whom we have interactions—especially those outside the church—should find us reasonable and big-hearted toward others.

A Gentle Reminder

As you drive away from your church after the Sunday morning service, do you ever look around at the neighborhood and say to yourself: I wonder what the folks here think about us? They see us pull into the church lot on Sunday morning, get out of our cars, perhaps wave hello to one another, and then step inside behind closed doors for a couple hours. Then we all spill out onto the pavement, get in our cars, and leave.

What are they thinking? What impression do they have of us? I wonder about this sometimes.

As I read Philippians 4:5, I get a clear picture of what our neighbors should see in us—what our reputation should be. Here's how Paul puts it: "Let your gentleness be evident to all." It seems clear that he is suggesting that this "gentleness" is not to be evident just to the folks with whom they attend church at Philippi, but "to all"—it must move beyond the church doors and out into the community.

Is your church known for gentleness? Bible teacher William Hendricksen fleshes this out for us nicely by giving a series of possible synonyms for *gentleness* as Paul used it here. What a helpful checklist this is for a body that worships together and has as its mission the proclamation of Jesus Christ and His love and salvation to the community.

Forbearance: Are we willing to be patient with others?

Yieldedness: Do we yield to our Lord, to biblical authority, to those God has put in charge? Do we yield our preferences for the good of the larger group?

Geniality: Does a warm friendliness permeate our presence?

Kindliness: In both word and action, are we kind?

Sweet reasonableness: Do we want the carpet to be the color we like? The music the style we prefer? Or are we reasonable with our fellow sinners who have been forgiven—just like us?

Considerateness: Do we, as Paul already pointed out, think of others over ourselves?

Charitableness: Where does charity start? May it start in our hearts and propel us into loving action toward others.

Mildness: The world is already harsh enough on the outside. Let's construct an oasis of mild in our church family.

Magnanimity: Big word that simply means we open our hearts to all to show them the hugeness of God's love.

Generosity: How can we not be generous since all we have is directly from our Father anyway?

There's a little of each of these things in the word Paul used and which is translated *gentleness*. Do our friends and neighbors see enough of these qualities in us to want to investigate why we are that way?

How Does This Verse Help Me Stand Firm?

To stand firm takes courage. It takes determination. It sometimes even takes stubbornness. But in standing firm, does my gentleness seep out a little as well? Do folks see me as caring, loving, patient? Or am I living in a way that reinforces the popular view that Christians are a bunch of snarly, defiant, you-better-be-like-us-or-else kind of folks? Firm but gentle wins the race.

What Has to Change?

What is my reputation at work? Do I exhibit any gentleness there? What is my reputation in the neighborhood? Strident or caring?

PHILIPPIANS 4:5–6

The Lord is near. Do not be anxious about anything,
but in every situation, by prayer and petition,
with thanksgiving, present your requests to God.

What You Need to Know

The simple, declarative sentence that introduces this passage—"The Lord is near"—is a bit of a conundrum for people who are trying to figure out exactly what Paul is saying. In fact, there are two possible meanings for Paul's statement, and both of them might be in play here. First, there is the literal meaning—that is, the Lord is near to us, or close by. Indeed that is true, because we know that our God is present in our lives through the Holy Spirit, and we have ongoing close personal contact with the Lord through prayer. Second, this passage could mean that in eschatological terms the return of the Lord is imminent— or possible at any time. We cannot categorically say which Paul has in mind. But here's some good news: It doesn't matter, for both are true. Our Lord is near—a prayer away or a trumpet call away. And those assurances add to our reason not to "be anxious about anything."

How Well Is It?

Peace is one of the most elusive qualities sought by those who are enduring life's difficult times. That is why I have long been amazed by the words of Horatio G. Spafford in his signature song "It Is Well with My Soul."

Mr. Spafford wrote the amazing words of that song of peace, tradition tells us, as he was on his way by ship to England. His ship was following a similar path to the one his wife, Anna, and their four daughters had taken just a few days earlier. But their ship was struck by another vessel, and many aboard lost their lives, including their girls.

Maggie. Bessie. Annie. Tanetta.

Gone.

My heart breaks for those parents every time I think about it. Having lost one teenage daughter, Melissa, to a sudden death in a car accident, I cannot imagine compounding our grief and distress by a multiple of four.

Aboard his ship, which was carrying him toward a sad reunion with his wife, Horatio Spafford penned these words:

When peace like a river attendeth my way,
When sorrows like sea billows roll;
Whatever my lot, Thou has taught me to say,
"It is well, it is well with my soul."

I have done a lot of thinking about this song—these words—since it was played at our daughter's funeral. Is it indeed possible when being stared down by tragedy or sadness or trouble to experience peace instead of anxiety? And if so, how? What words of Scripture can make this promise for us?

From my own experience, it seems that to find peace in the midst of roiling sea billows, we need two things—both promised in Philippians 4:5–6:

1. We need God's presence: "The Lord is near" (v. 5). Often when hard times hit, we turn our back on God in anger. But as difficult as it sometimes sounds, we need to be like David in the Psalms. While he offered plenty of complaints about a number of issues, after he expressed his feelings, he turned to God for help (see Psalm 10:1, 16–17 for example).

It is when life is hardest and God seems the most distant or the most mysterious that we need to be the most intentional about basking in His presence—to feel the warmth of Paul's words: "The Lord is near." Just as any problem feels a bit less troublesome when a loved one extends a hand or wraps us in arms of love, so do we gain peace when we realize that God is near to cover us with His protection.

2. We need to replace anxiety with trust: "Do not be anxious about anything, but in every situation, by prayer and petition, with thanksgiving, present your requests to God" (v. 6). The Lord tells us clearly, "Cast all your anxiety on [Me]" (1 Peter 5:7), and the best way to accomplish that is through prayer.

In another passage we learn from Paul how this happens. When he had been in jail in Philippi on an earlier occasion (Acts 16), Paul, along with his friend Silas, spent their nighttime praying and singing. They were casting their anxiety on the Lord through prayer, and on this occasion God answered through an earthquake and a mini-revival among the jail workers. Peace replaced anxiety when Paul trusted God.

We may never experience anything that approximates what Horatio and Anna Spafford went through back in 1873, but if we want the peace he describes in his great hymn, our challenge is to listen to Paul and learn from his words and his example. Then it can be well with our soul.

How Do These Verses Help Me Stand Firm?

Suppose that in the midst of struggles and difficulties I clam up in my connection to God—I ignore His nearness and refuse to speak with Him about my troubles. If I do that, I have no prospect for peace. This passage helps me know how to avoid that darkness.

What Has to Change?

Am I relishing God's nearness or am I pushing Him away? Am I taking advantage of the chance to speak with Him and pour out my heart-cry for help to Him? If not, I need to change my response.

PHILIPPIANS 4:7

And the peace of God, which transcends all understanding,
will guard your hearts and your minds in Christ Jesus.

What You Need to Know

Philippi was a city living under Roman occupation, so the people knew what it meant to have soldiers at the ready, guarding them. They would have understood Paul's use of the word *guard* from their own experience: God's transcendent, inexplicable peace would stand like a Roman guard over their hearts and minds.

The Search for Peace

Picture this scene. You are on vacation. Before you left your house, you put every possible thing in order. You made sure the newspapers were not going to pile up on your doorstep. You had the post office hold your mail. Your house was secure, and you even made sure the garage door was closed before you drove away.

At work, you made sure all your projects were completed or covered by someone else.

You had paid all your bills in advance, and before you took off for your vacation you made sure all of your travel and lodging arrangements were in order.

Finally, you got to your vacation spot—let's say a house on the beach—and everything was perfect.

The first day of your vacation, the sun was shining, the water was glistening, and your favorite book was in hand. You left your cell phone in the house and you parked yourself on the beach for a day of nothing but relaxation.

Now, that is peace. That is a peace we all understand. We know why it works, and we all long for that kind of calming, relaxing peace once in a while. We may not get enough of it in our lives, but we all recognize it and understand it.

The apostle Paul, writing in a house in Rome that was anything but a vacation spot, and writing from a perspective that was anything but beach scenes and lapping waves, had a totally different kind of peace in mind for us.

This is not vacation peace. This is godly peace. This is a peace that we absolutely cannot understand. Indeed, it is a peace that "transcends human understanding" as J. B. Phillips put it in translating this verse.

Consider for a moment what happens when we face trouble or anxiety. How easy is it to think during those times? How clear is our understanding when we are under duress? Not so good, right?

But when God's peace comes to calm us and comfort us, it offers us an incomprehensible protection. And this protection will "guard [our] hearts and [our] minds in Christ Jesus."

Nothing that psychology or logic or humanity's reasoning offers can match what God offers with His transcendent understanding. When we turn our situation over to Him, freeing ourselves of the burdens by heartfelt prayer, God replaces what could weigh down our thinking with a divine understanding that offers us a protection only our Savior can provide.

And that is peace.

That is a peace that outshines the best day under a palm tree on the beach.

How Does This Verse Help Me Stand Firm?

Who does not want peace? Who does not want safety? How much firmer can I stand than to have a promise from my divine, holy God to give me both? The only thing left is to accept this offer and to let the Father hold me up, on legs made wobbly by trouble, and see His peace calm my broken heart.

What Has to Change?

Am I depending more on my own abilities to negotiate difficulties than I am on the abilities of my sovereign Lord? Am I willing to let God be my heart's guard?

PHILIPPIANS 4:8

*Finally, brothers and sisters, whatever is true,
whatever is noble, whatever is right, whatever is pure,
whatever is lovely, whatever is admirable—if anything
is excellent or praiseworthy—think about such things.*

What You Need to Know

"What's the greatest commandment?" Jesus was once asked. His response? "Love the Lord your God with all your heart and with all your soul and with all your mind" (Matthew 22:37).

Faith is not something ethereal and mystical. It is real. And it requires mindful love—a desire to please God not just with the soul but also with the mental capacities He has given us. Christian faith should be a cerebral activity, not a mindless religion given to chanting or following rote traditions or numb repetitions. The mind must be engaged at all times in loving God. And in this passage, Paul—well-educated and cultured and well-traveled— gives us a lesson in what that mind dedicated to the Lord should "think about."

Peace Plan

Why is there no peace?

Our world seems wracked by anger, by disappointment, by despair, by conflict. We can act as if it doesn't exist or we don't see it, but the headlines on any news website tell us otherwise. Just take a look at the string of headlines for one day on CNN's site, in actual order as they appeared on the day I wrote this:

Bullies
Suicide
People Missing
Murder Suspect
Projected Job Cuts
Reasons for a Murder
Unemployment
Huge Firm May Owe You Money (finally, some good news)
Workplace Immorality
And on it goes.

In a world in which everyone seems to want what the beauty queens always want—World Peace—there seems to be little of it.

But how can there be in a world that is bent on rejecting the Prince of Peace and His words that promise peace?

The apostle Paul, as earlier noted, prescribed individual peace by suggesting the importance of God's presence, of turning anxieties over to the Lord, and of praying and petitioning for help. Yet he is not done explaining the elements that bring peace in our lives. He seems to be sandwiching his two mentions of peace (vv. 7, 9) with several practical suggestions for how we are to live if we want to have the inner peace that leads to a godly life.

As we look around at our world, it's not hard to see that many of our problems could be avoided by letting our minds dwell on the seven ideals Paul sets forth. Let's see if that makes sense.

Think about what is true.

I recall Dr. James Grier, one of my favorite college professors (I talked about him in my discussion of Philippians 3:12), reminding us over and over about the importance of what he called "Capital T Truth." He was referring to God's Word, and he wanted us to remember that no matter what else the world might throw our way, we could always depend on God's inspired Word to be true and to be our guide for faith and practice in life. (Sadly that ideal is eroding, even in Christian circles.)

What is true is what God says is true. God created the heavens and the earth. Man fell because he was deceived. God promised a plan to redeem man. God established a family to carry a lineage from ancient times through to the time of Jesus' birth, which was prophesied in the Old Testament. Jesus was incarnation of God himself, and He set aside His glories of heaven to live here, die here, and rise from the dead so our salvation could be secure. God gave us guidelines for living in His inspired book.

That is truth. That is what we need to think about.

Think about what is noble.

Nobility—dignity, decency, goodness—is often scoffed at today. Sarcasm and sardonic comments seem to have won the day. It's time to rebuild noble thinking into our consciousness. Ruth, for example, was honored for being of "noble character" in the way she interacted with men (Ruth 3:11). The woman of Proverbs 31 was honored for nobility—for being a strong, determined businesswoman and a wise mother. Isaiah 32:8 honors the noble man for making "noble plans." Consider how nobility might change how you look at life and how others look at you.

Think about what is right.

"Righteousness guards the person of integrity" (Proverbs 13:6). Nobody needs to have a degree in theology to know what is righteous and what is not. These are things informed by Holy Spirit-directed wisdom and carried through by careful decision-making. Thinking right leads away from living wrong.

Think about what is pure.

Repeat after the psalmist: "Create in me a pure heart, O God" (51:10). Purity is right desire combined with controlled action. Doing comes from thinking, and pure thinking results in pure activities. This is godliness lived out without shame or regret.

Think about what is lovely.

The Greek word that is translated *lovely* here is reserved for this use alone in the New Testament. In most Bible versions, *lovely* is the translation of choice. But in *The Message*, Eugene Peterson selected the word *compelling*. Interesting choice. We are compelled by what attracts us—what is interesting to us—and what intrigues us. If we are to think about those kinds of things—minus anything that is impure—our thoughts must move toward that which holds high interest and intellectual stimulation for us. We can be compelled by great art or by advancements in medicine or great discoveries in astronomy—the sky is the limit. God has given us the ability and the freedom to use our minds to examine the compelling things of this world.

Think about what is admirable, excellent, or praiseworthy.

Consider the media and what it offers us today. What if we carried around in our heads this mental checklist for what we allow to brighten our screens—computer, TV, iPhones?

Is it to be admired?

Is it excellent?

Is it worthy of praise?

It's worth using our minds to consider, isn't it?

How Does This Verse Help Me Stand Firm?

If ever there was a problem stopper in my life, this verse is it. A firm stand for Jesus—a life lived with cross-carrying excellence—is marked by these traits.

What Has to Change?

What occupies my mind? Do I love the Lord with my mind so much that I want these traits to be my guidelines?

PHILIPPIANS 4:9

Whatever you have learned or received or heard from me, or seen in me— put it into practice. And the God of peace will be with you.

What You Need to Know

This is not the first time Paul has set up himself as a worthy and respected example. In 1 Corinthians 11, he says this—and his qualifier makes all the difference: "Follow my example, as I follow the example of Christ" (v. 1). Jesus is the primary example to follow, and at any level at which Paul has mirrored the Savior, we can mirror the apostle. We emulate human leaders or teachers or preachers or others only to the extent that they live Christlike lives. That's important to realize as we check out Paul's teaching here.

Who to Follow

Paul was not perfect. In fact, the great apostle said that when it came to sinners "I am the worst" (1 Timothy 1:15). He also said that sometimes he did things that he wished he hadn't done (Romans 7:15), and that, as he put it, "good itself does not dwell in me."

Paul was painfully honest about himself. He knew that despite Jesus' work in his life, he was not perfect. He knew that even though he went around the known world spreading the seed of the gospel like a first-century Johnny Appleseed, he was not beyond the reach of the Devil's wiles.

Yet look at what he is telling us here: "Whatever you have learned or received or heard from me, or seen in me—put it into practice." If all we knew about Paul was that he was the worst of sinners and that he couldn't help himself from doing wrong, we might want to rethink this offer. But two things help us understand how valuable this advice is.

First, we remember that all of those things that might drag Paul down are things we are susceptible to as well. We are tempted and we are sometimes torn—pulled by the world, the flesh, and the Devil. In that regard, we know that Paul is one of us, not some holier-than-thou figurehead who pretends to be perfect.

And then there is this. Paul has already explained the standard by which we can decide when to follow his example. Those all-important words are found in his letter to the church in Corinth. In 1 Corinthians 11:1, Paul tells those brother and sisters: "Follow my example as I follow the example of Christ." It was only in the times and the circumstances when Paul lived according to the supreme example, Christ, that the folks in Philippi were to follow him.

Now, that might leave us with a bit of a problem if we take Paul literally, because he is not here anymore for us to follow. He did not visit our church in its infancy as he did Philippi, and he is not sending us a personal note hand-delivered by someone we love and trust. We are getting this note of example secondhand, and we have no chance to observe Paul in action. How do we model our activity, then, after Paul?

We must understand what Christlike living is all about. To do that, we study our Savior to see what characteristics He demonstrated for us while He dusted His sandals on earthly roads. Not to discount what Paul was telling his friends, but we have an opportunity to bypass the middleman on this. Sure, we can learn much from studying Paul's writings in the New Testament. But as 1 Peter 2:21 indicates, it is Jesus we are to emulate.

It is His compassion that should mark our lives.

It is His willingness to serve rather than to be served that should characterize our attitude.

It is His striving to do the Father's will that should inform our lives.

It is His prayerfulness that should guide our relationship with God.

It is His love for sinners that should energize our witness.

It is His concern for the less fortunate that should break our hearts.

Paul set an example for his friends in what he taught, in what he gave, in what he said, and in what he demonstrated. And as much as we can look over his shoulder in Scripture to see what those things might be, we should learn from them. But the primary person we are to follow—as did Paul—is our Savior.

When we study Jesus' example and then incorporate Christlikeness into our lives, we can gain the same advantage the

Philippians did by following Paul: "The God of peace" will be with us (4:9).

What a promise! By living the right way, the Jesus way, we not only gain the distinct advantages of holiness but we also enjoy the calm comfort of a life of peace. Is there anything better than that?

How Does This Verse Help Me Stand Firm?

What a challenge this is, for it sets up for me the possibility that I could be that good example, as Paul was. As I stand firm, I allow others to look at me as a positive role model from whom they can learn.

What Has to Change?

Would I want anyone to live as I live and then look back, point to me, and say, "I followed his/her example?" What have I done in the past week that has been, or has not been, worthy of emulating?

PHILIPPIANS 4:10–11

I rejoiced greatly in the Lord that at last you renewed your concern for me. Indeed, you were concerned, but you had no opportunity to show it. I am not saying this because I am in need, for I have learned to be content whatever the circumstances.

What You Need to Know

In all of the New Testament there is only one occurrence of the word translated "content" in Philippians 4:11. It is a Greek word, of course, *autarkes*. According to Thayer, it means "sufficient for one's self, strong enough to need no aid or support."

When Paul used this word, his readers or listeners would have known that he was alluding to the philosophy of Stoicism—man's self-sufficiency despite the circumstances. But they would have soon seen (in verse 13) that what Paul was describing was not self-caused: it came from Christ and His strength. This would have been an important distinction, for Stoicism was not founded on God's truth but on a secular way of thinking.

> Paul may have captured the attention of his readers with this reference to a popular philosophy, but he clarified what he meant in verse 13—not self but Christ.

Jail Talk

Over the years I have received many letters from people in prison. In most cases, they have read something I have written in *Our Daily Bread,* and they want to either discuss it with me or tell me that the words helped them. Many of them know that our family has suffered a devastating loss, so they sense that I will have compassion for what they are going through.

What I am most impressed by when I get these letters is the occasional writer who shares with me that despite his location and his living conditions, he has found security and contentment in Jesus Christ. From what I have seen of prisons, it would not be easy to hang the word *contentment* on the incarcerated life. So this kind of jail talk impresses me, and when I write back to these brothers in Christ, I tell them so.

Having heard from these men helps me understand just a little better what Paul is talking about in Philippians 4:10–11. Certainly his words were "jail talk," for he was under arrest and confined to a house in Rome. So for him to talk about being content is impressive.

But there is so much more to Paul's life than jail. And some of it is even worse.

When he says "whatever the circumstances," he's not saying, "Oh, yeah, and whatever." He's lived the "whatever." Let's take a look at some of what Paul endured:

- Not just one incarceration, but several.
- He was flogged.
- He was often on the verge of death.
- He had a "thorn in the flesh" that God refused to remove.
- On three occasions he was beaten with rods.
- He was shipwrecked three times.
- Thieves threatened him.
- Gentiles were upset with him.
- He suffered many sleepless nights.
- People lied to him about faith matters.
- He had been hungry, naked, and cold.

And we think we have problems because the drain plugs up, the car goes "ka-thunk, ka-thunk," the kids didn't make the right soccer team, our job isn't as much fun as we think it should be, we don't have enough money for a new hot tub, or our church isn't perfect.

After all that he had experienced, Paul could say, "I have learned to be content." And he could still "[rejoice] greatly in the Lord."

Have we learned to exist contentedly within our circumstances, whatever they may be? What a difference in our lives when we find contentment that helps us resist the urge to sink into despair when things don't go our way. When we do, God is glorified and His name is honored.

How Do These Verses Help Me Stand Firm?

If I am trying to stand firm on the foundation of society's standards—houses, good jobs, great locations, that kind of thing—my foundation will shift depending on the circumstances. It's not easy to put myself totally in the hands of God and seek His will in every situation—always with a good attitude. But that seems to be what Paul is talking about here.

What Has to Change?

How do I face difficulties with realism yet without despair? Do I live out a contentment that glorifies the Lord?

PHILIPPIANS 4:12–13

I know what it is to be in need, and I know what it is to have plenty. I have learned the secret of being content in any and every situation, whether well fed or hungry, whether living in plenty or in want. I can do all this through him who gives me strength.

What You Need to Know

I wonder how many people would keep going in the ministry if they had to put up with what Paul put up with? Let's look at what he's talking about when he says, "I know what it is to be in need."

Acts 14:19: "They stoned Paul and dragged him outside the city, thinking he was dead." Left for dead? That's being in need.

Acts 16:22–23: "The crowd joined in the attack against Paul and Silas, and the magistrates ordered them to be stripped and beaten with rods. After they had been severely flogged, they were thrown into prison." Humiliated, beaten with rods? Thrown into jail? That's being in need.

Acts 20:3: "Because the Jews had plotted against [Paul] just as he was about to sail for Syria, he decided to go back through Macedonia." Being plotted against? That's being in need.

2 Corinthians 11:27: "I have labored and toiled and have often gone without sleep; I have known hunger and thirst and have often gone without food; I have been cold and naked." Sleeplessness, hunger, thirst, nakedness? That's being in need.

Those were the circumstances Paul was able to "do" through his Savior's strength. Those are needs we may never have to experience, but we have our own list. How are we doing with our list?

I Can Do Anything! Or Not

For many years I was privileged to be in charge of a Christian sports magazine. Our task was to find the top Christian sports people and feature them in our pages. Along the way, I was able to interview a number of those athletes and coaches both for the magazine and for several books I wrote.

As we talked to these sluggers or pitchers or quarterbacks or point guards or goalies, we discovered that the most popular favorite verse among them was Philippians 4:13: "I can do all this through him who gives me strength." It seemed to be the perfect go-to passage for men and women who had to compete at the highest levels.

"All this" fits neatly into their theology, because you can even put baseball in there if you want. And it offers the key component that all athletes need: "strength." What better verse is there for a struggling second baseman who can't seem to get a base hit than, "I can do all things, even hit a 90-mile-an-hour fastball, in the power of One who provides the strength." I'm not criticizing them or even downplaying the value of this passage for all of us, but this sports element does force us to look deeper into this passage to see what Paul really means.

The first key to understanding how to apply this verse, then, is figuring out what Paul means by "all things." Is there a specific connection that we must use, or can we apply "all things" across the board to whatever we attempt to do? Does Jesus (the understood "him" of the passage), according to this verse, help us write that poem we want to write, get that job we desire, change the oil in our car, win the lottery, marry the girl of our dreams, hit a home run with the bases loaded?

Paul, in his suggestion that he "can do all things," is referring back to verse 12, in which he says that he knows how to live "in need" and he knows how to live "in plenty." He can do life when he doesn't know where his next meal is coming from, and he can do life when he has moments of comfort and ease (which didn't seem to happen too often for Paul).

But then he introduces the second key, which takes this out of the realm of self-congratulations and puts it into the realm of God-sufficiency. Paul says he can do those things "through Christ," or "in Christ" as some versions put it. This is the secret to contentment Paul is talking about. If he were to crawl into the shelter of God's protection or to depend totally on God's power or to rely completely on the Lord—in other words, to live in the "strength of the one who lives within me" (Phillips)—he would be enabled to find contentment. He would be able to do "all things" or to thrive in every situation.

In effect, Paul was saying to life: Bring it on. I am ready for anything as long as I face the situation in the power and strength of my almighty provider.

In 2 Corinthians 12:9, Paul quoted Jesus, who said, "My grace is sufficient for you, for my power is made perfect in weakness." God's grace and God's power—even in the weakness we feel in our circumstances—are the reasons that we don't have to do life feeling threatened or defeated.

No matter what the situation—whether we find ourselves in need or in ease—we can deal with it only because we have the power of Christ in our lives. That's what Paul is talking about here, and that has so much more value in our lives than the ability to run a 100-meter dash faster than anyone else.

How is your life? Whatever the circumstance, you can do it—in Christ.

How Do These Verses Help Me Stand Firm?

How often do I attempt to do the work of God on my own—depending on my power of persuasion or my glib tongue or my perceived salesmanship to get the job done? When I do that, I am really just displaying my weakness. Instead, I need to allow the Lord to overcome my weakness and show His power.

What Has to Change?

Today when I began my day, did I see Christ's strength—or did I just plow into the day on my own? What are some of the "all this" that I need to start doing in God's power?

PHILIPPIANS 4:14–18

Yet it was good of you to share in my troubles. Moreover, as you Philippians know, in the early days of your acquaintance with the gospel, when I set out from Macedonia, not one church shared with me in the matter of giving and receiving, except you only; for even when I was in Thessalonica, you sent me aid more than once when I was in need. Not that I desire your gifts; what I desire is that more be credited to your account. I have received full payment and have more than enough. I am amply supplied, now that I have received from Epaphroditus the gifts you sent. They are a fragrant offering, an acceptable sacrifice, pleasing to God.

What You Need to Know

Paul waxes nostalgic as this passage begins. He's saying, in effect, "You might remember when I was just getting started . . ." and goes on to talk about the tough days when he had little support on his mission. This mission is what we call Paul's second missionary journey (Acts 16:12–40).

A Fragrant Offering

When my wife and I were just out of college, we felt God's call to go to the Philippines to teach at a missionary kids' school outside of Manila. In fact, it was exciting how that call developed. I was in the Philippines playing on an evangelistic college basketball team when I first visited the school. This being long before texting and e-mails, I mailed a letter to Sue telling her that I thought God was prompting us to return to that school to teach. As my letter journeyed toward our apartment in Ohio, it crossed paths with a letter I received from her in which she told me that she felt God's clear leading that we should go to the Philippines—something we had never discussed. Needless to say, we were soon making plans to go.

Just as exciting as our call was the amazing support we received for our missionary venture. Three churches—the one I grew up in, the one Sue grew up in, and the one we attended as a couple in Ohio—provided our entire support. You can imagine how encouraging it was to us as a young couple to see these three bodies of believers trust us so much that they took care of all of our financial needs so we could work with those remarkable missionary kids at Faith Academy.

That's why I am so touched by the words of Paul in this passage. He was thanking the Philippians because, as he put it, "You sent me aid more than once when I was in need" (4:16). I know that feeling of being loved and cared for and trusted and depended on by fellow believers—men and women who are willing to open up their checkbooks to support those God calls to His work away from home.

Unlike Sue and me, Paul did not have a multiplicity of churches that gave him aid. He had just the Philippi church. We don't know why that is, but we can assume that the others had not matured yet to the point of understanding the value of giving. And while it seems that some churches had rejected this opportunity, we can assume this one thing was true: Those churches that did not give—that held back for whatever reason—missed a huge blessing.

I know that when we returned to our three churches after our year in the Philippines, we were greeted warmly and openly. These folks knew that what they had done for us was valuable for God's kingdom, and they benefited by having helped us. They learned the grace of giving, and we felt such a bond of fellowship with them because of their allowing us to have a fantastic year of ministry.

I like what Paul said to the church: "Not that I desire your gifts; what I desire is that more be credited to your account" (v. 17). Whenever we as a body of believers or we as individuals contribute to God's work, we are making an investment in something that pays huge spiritual dividends.

When we invest our dollars in a woman who is working with inner-city youth, we are investing in lives that are changed when they hear the gospel.

When we invest our dollars in a couple working in Papua New Guinea, we are investing in lives of people who might never have otherwise heard the gospel.

When we invest in the lives of a family that is working with youth in Ukraine, we are giving opportunity for eternal change to kids who might otherwise be lost.

And as we do, we are a tremendous blessing to those who receive the funds. Those gifts we give are "a fragrant offering, an acceptable sacrifice, pleasing to God."

How Do These Verses Help Me Stand Firm?

As part of the body of believers worldwide, I stand with more certainty and power when I stand together with others. My giving and my prayers for fellow believers worldwide help create a grid of sustenance that allows God's work to flourish. The more I help others stand strong in their mission, the firmer I stand in mine.

What Has to Change?

Who needs my help in the worldwide work of the Lord? Who needs me to be a prayer warrior as they seek to spread the gospel? Who out there in the field of the Lord needs encouragement from me via e-mail or letter or tweet?

PHILIPPIANS 4:19–20

And my God will meet all your needs according to the riches of his glory in Christ Jesus. To our God and Father be glory for ever and ever.

What You Need to Know

What do you get from the Man who has everything? That seems to be the idea in this passage, for when we speak of the riches of Jesus Christ, the treasure chest is endless. Jesus possesses all things. Therefore, there is no end to the supply of His provisions. And He loves to provide, because in doing so, His glory is shown to us. His unsearchable riches reflect glory on our God and Father—and we are a part of that when God meets our needs according to His infinite riches.

My God

Three little words are coming off the lips and fingertips of so many today: "Oh, my God!" This sacrilegious and flippant expression has become so prevalent that it has been abbreviated to three letters for texting purposes. And it has become the three-word motto of almost everyone who expresses surprise—from game show winners to reality show participants to little children who see something that has captured their attention.

And it is safe to assume that most people are uttering those words with no regard for our heavenly Father at all. To them, using His name as a slang expression of surprise or even disgust has no more meaning than saying "Wow" or "Oh, phooey!"

These words, though, compose a precious, glorious expression of honor to the One who loves us and sustains our very existence. It is also a personal expression of our relationship with Him. When we say, "My God," we are telling the world that we have a warm connection to the greatest Being in the universe. He is not just some distant, unattached God. He is my very own personal, loving, caring, and interested God. He is not just "the God" out there in some impersonal theological existence. He is mine, and I am His. He is "my God," we are saying, and those words mean "I love Him with an indescribable and inter-related love."

That's a lot to think about when we begin to read Philippians 4:19–20, but it is vital to an understanding of what is going on here.

Paul, who had just commended his friends in Philippi for meeting his missionary needs despite their own apparent poverty (2 Corinthians 8:2–3 seems to indicate this), is about to give this church some incredibly good news: He has a personal Friend in high places who will take care of whatever needs they might have.

"My God," Paul says—reminding them of his one-to-one connection to his heavenly Father—"will meet all your needs."

Just as they met Paul's needs, His God—who was, of course, their God too—would meet theirs.

When they found a deficit in their financial situation, God's love and care would help them survive.

When they discovered themselves struggling physically, in their weakness God could make them strong.

When they felt bankrupt spiritually, God would build them up and restore their relationship with Him.

And how is this going to happen? What is Paul's assurance that his God can do this? Because he has seen what Jesus can do. When he tells the Philippians that his God will supply their needs "according to the riches of his glory in Christ Jesus," Paul knows what he is talking about. He has experienced firsthand how Jesus can change a life—his. He has experienced firsthand how Jesus can save a man from all kinds of dangers. And he has seen Jesus' glory firsthand, as he explained in 2 Corinthians 4:6: "For God who said, 'Let light shine out of darkness,' made his light shine in our hearts to give us the light of the knowledge of God's glory displayed in the face of Christ."

Paul knew the glorious riches of Christ, and he knew he could tell his friends that His God would take care of them out of God's abundant wealth.

Can we see how puny our misdirected "Oh, my God" sounds now when we use those words to describe some trinket of life?

When we realize what our God, who promised in Psalm 23 that we "shall not want," has done for us in meeting all of our needs, our response should mirror Paul's when he said, "To our God and Father be glory for ever and ever. Amen." Those are the words "My God" deserves to hear from us. That is the doxology of our appreciation to an eternal, all-knowing, all-powerful God who has stooped to care for us and unburden our hearts with His glorious riches.

How Do These Verses Help Me Stand Firm?

Unless I have a full and right view of God and His supply of riches in my life, I don't have all of the resources I need to stand firm. My God—your God—can meet my greatest need.

What Has to Change?

Do I ever use our great provider God's name in a flippant or disrespectful way? Can I limit my references to God to only those times when I worship His awesomeness and in every way recognize His majesty?

PHILIPPIANS 4:21–22

Greet all God's people in Christ Jesus. The brothers and sisters who are with me send greetings. All God's people here send you greetings, especially those who belong to Caesar's household.

What You Need to Know

At this point in other letters Paul wrote to the churches, he took the stylus and the "paper" and penned his own note as his personal greeting to his friends. In 2 Thessalonians 3:17 he said, "I, Paul, write this greeting in my own hand, which is the distinguishing mark in all my letters." So, there is some evidence here that these words, "Greet all God's people . . . " could have been written by Paul's own hand.

Dear Everybody:

Did you ever write a letter to a group of people—perhaps a family—in which you were careful not to leave anyone out? You mentioned everyone's name, both on your side of the letter and on the receiving side, so that everyone could be a part of the correspondence. So that no one would feel left out or dissatisfied?

Paul does something similar as he wraps up his letter to his friends at Philippi. But he does this without mentioning any names.

First, he directs his note toward each believer who might hear this letter read. As the New King James states it, "Greet every saint in Christ Jesus." This is a little more personal than the way the NIV translates it: "Greet all God's people." Paul wants "every" single fellow Christian in the church to be greeted.

"Hello, Marcus, from Paul."

"Lydia, Paul says hi."

"Eunice, the apostle sends his greetings."

Imagine how warmly those greetings would have been accepted.

But these were not just ordinary greetings. They were delivered "in Christ Jesus"—in the name of the Savior. Not as a magical incantation but as a reminder of Jesus' love and sacrifice, which is what drew these people together into a family in the first place. The limiting factor of being "in Christ Jesus" is both a badge of honor and a challenge to live up to His name.

The second group mentioned in Paul's final greeting relates to the fellow believers Paul was familiar with in Rome. It reminds me of one of those times when your family is on vacation and you call or Skype to talk to a parent or other loved ones back home. Everyone gathers around the computer and jockeys for position to say hello to Grandma or whoever is receiving the call. That feeling of family and bonding is solidified if everyone has a chance to be a part of the greeting.

For Paul, who valued the idea that Jews and Gentiles, bond and free, male and female could worship Jesus together, this would have been a special message. It would have said to the people of Philippi that there were fellow believers among the Romans—or whoever was represented by "the brothers and sisters who are with me." It wouldn't matter, really, what their background might have been. They were family.

And then the third group: "especially those who belong to Caesar's household." Paul's mention of this group is somewhat mysterious—were these members of Caesar's family or were they servants in Caesar's house? Whatever the case, the implication is that these were brothers and sisters in Christ and thus should be included in this greeting from the family of believers in Rome.

Paul was inclusive in his greetings and in who he mentioned. Could that be a hint to us that we should show concern and love for all around us—whatever their background? Paul's display of unity should point us toward finding common ground with others—even those outside our normal circle.

May God find us compassionate and concerned for "all the saints" in God's kingdom—praying for, caring for, and loving the wide fellowship of men and women who have put their faith in the finished work of Jesus Christ.

How Do These Verses Help Me Stand Firm?

Paul's greetings can awaken me to my need to show Christian love toward all believers instead of narrowing my world to just those I know really well. Who knows, perhaps I might find someone new at work or in my neighborhood with whom I can fellowship in the Savior.

What Has to Change?

Am I content to stick to my closed circle of Christian friends? Would it be to my spiritual benefit to widen my search for fellow Christ-followers? Could I perhaps even accomplish something new and powerful in His name if I were to do this?

PHILIPPIANS 4:23

*The grace of the Lord Jesus Christ
be with your spirit: Amen.*

What You Need to Know

Let's take a look at how Paul ended his letters throughout the New Testament. It'll be pretty clear that there is a pattern here.

1 Corinthians: "The grace of the Lord Jesus be with you. My love to all of you in Christ Jesus. Amen."

2 Corinthians: "May the grace of the Lord Jesus Christ, and the love of God, and the fellowship of the Holy Spirit be with you all."

Galatians: "The grace of our Lord Jesus Christ be with your spirit, brothers and sisters. Amen."

Ephesians: "Grace to all who love our Lord Jesus Christ with an undying love."

Philippians: "The grace of the Lord Jesus Christ be with your spirit. Amen."

Colossians and 1 Timothy: "Grace be with you."

1 and 2 Thessalonians: "The grace of our Lord Jesus Christ be with you." (Add the word all to the end for 2 Thessalonians.)

2 Timothy: "The Lord be with your spirit. Grace be with you."

Titus: "Grace be with you all."

Philemon: "The grace of the Lord Jesus Christ be with your spirit."

Bookends of Grace

When I teach writing on the college level, I talk to my students about their introductions and their conclusions. I tell them how important it is to get the reader's attention at the beginning with a good introduction and to let them go at the end with a satisfying conclusion.

One method I recommend is to combine the two in what I call bookends. In this style, the introduction and the conclusion share a common image or picture, which is pleasing to readers because they sense a feeling of completion.

Paul must have heard one of my lectures.

At the beginning of this letter to his friends in Philippi, after his typical greeting, he said, "Grace and peace to you" (1:2). And now, after he has run through a number of vital Christian living issues with them, he ends his epistle with similar words: "The grace of the Lord Jesus Christ be with your spirit" (4:23).

Since Paul begins with grace and talks about it in the middle of the letter as well, it makes sense that there is nothing more important to leave his readers with than another challenge toward grace. And interestingly, he wants grace to be with their spirit.

This is more than a nice benediction. Think of what it means for grace to be with our spirit. This goes beyond knowing about grace. Having grace in our spirit, it seems to me, is a challenge to have grace informing every part of our lives.

A situation comes up as we deal with someone at work. Perhaps this person has slighted us or even insulted us. This can make every day a chore as we face that person. But if grace is in our spirit, working to temper our reaction and to control our thinking, maybe we can find a graceful, kind way to respond to this person. An attitude of grace might just turn what could be a daily distraction or even an ongoing hurt into an opportunity to show Christlike love.

Grace in our spirit could surely help us in our family relationships. It is a lack of grace toward our loved ones—perhaps leading us to emphasize selfishness or harshness or misunderstanding—that tears families apart. Would it be fair to say that a surplus of spirit-grace has never caused a family to be in turmoil, but a lack of it is usually the trademark of a wounded home?

When the grace of the Lord Jesus is with our spirit, we can love the unlovely.

We can employ the grace in our spirit to turn the other cheek when an unkind word smacks us the wrong way.

We can use the power of Christ's grace to soldier through the pain when someone lets us down, recognizing how Jesus never drops us if we do the same to Him.

We can practice our Savior's grace to forgive that family member who seems bent on making self-destructive decisions.

No wonder Paul chooses this benediction time and time again in his letters. It is not just his instructions, as wise and godly as they are, that will change the people who get his letters.

It is not just his example, as shining as that is, that will make people follow in his footsteps as he asks them to do. It is not simply his practical call for an indescribable peace that will allow the people to pray aright and think aright and therefore live aright. All of these things must be accompanied by and empowered by the grace of the Lord Jesus Christ residing in and flowing out of the spirit of the redeemed.

This is not a throwaway line that Paul uses at the end of his letters. It is not just a great literary device. It is one last inspired word from God—one more admonition and challenge to His people. It is a final word that, if properly applied, can spur the reader to a life of value and purpose in the service of the King.

And so I, too, leave you with Paul's powerful, effective, God-breathed words, praying that this short benediction can make your life a showcase of God's grace, love, and mercy to everyone whose life you will touch: "The grace of the Lord Jesus Christ be with your spirit. Amen!"

How Does This Verse Help Me Stand Firm?

How appropriate is this reminder as I seek to stand firm in the love of Christ and in the knowledge of His Word! It is God's way of telling me that it is not about me and my personal efforts. It is through God's grace working with my spirit that I stand firm.

What Has to Change?

How does grace manifest itself in my life? Am I noted for graciousness in my response to others? Is there grace in my spirit in the midst of trials—grace that helps me shine Jesus' light on others?

ABOUT THE AUTHOR

After serving for eighteen years as managing editor of *Sports Spectrum* magazine, Dave became an editor for Discovery House Publishers. He is also a regular contributor to *Our Daily Bread*. A freelance writer for many years, he has authored sixteen books. Dave and his wife, Sue, love rollerblading and spending time with their children and grandchildren. Dave has enjoyed traveling with students on ministry trips to Jamaica, Alaska, and England.

NOTE TO THE READER

The publisher invites you to share your response to the message of this book by writing Discovery House, P.O. Box 3566, Grand Rapids, MI 49501, U.S.A. For information about other Discovery House books, music, or DVDs, contact us at the same address or call 1-800-653-8333. Find us online at dhp.org or send e-mail to books@dhp.org.